HEROIC

HEROIC

THE
SURPRISING PATH TO
TRUE MANHOOD

◆────────◆────────◆

BILL DELVAUX

PUBLISHING GROUP

NASHVILLE, TENNESSEE

Published by B&H Publishing Group
Nashville, Tennessee

Dewey Decimal Classification: 248.842
Subject Heading: HEROES AND HEROINES / MEN /
JESUS CHRIST

Cover illustration by Anthony Benedetto; Nova Nimbus.

1 2 3 4 5 6 7 • 22 21 20 19

To my brothers, Tom and John.
This one's for you.

ACKNOWLEDGMENTS

This book would have never been written without the prodding of Dave Schroeder and Phil Davis. It was your belief in me that pushed me to begin when I had little confidence in myself. I had to trust you to start. I am forever grateful.

I also have to say a huge thank you to the design team at B&H Publishing, to Jade Novak and Susan Browne. Your work with artist Anthony Benedetto gave birth to such compelling cover art.

Thank you to my editor, Taylor Combs, for astute suggestions on both style and content. You have made me a better writer.

Thank you to all the men at West End Community Church that listened to this material in a teaching format and gave helpful feedback.

Thanks to the Thursday morning group of men—to Ingle, Brian E., Randy, Matt, Brian L., Wes, and Bryan C. You first read the manuscript and shared your stories with me. I am thankful to be part of your lives.

Thanks to the board of Landmark Journey Ministries—to Ed, Scott Mc., Scott H., Rob, Adele, Phil, and Rick. You have been unwavering cheerleaders through all the ups and downs.

Thanks to the young men who did a final reading of the manuscript—to Marshall, Ashton, Matt, Justin, Nathan, and Grey. Your helpful suggestions helped me stay on course.

Thanks to my band of brothers—to Dave, Terry, Bill, and Howard. You have walked so many miles with me, encouraging me throughout the writing of this book. I hope we get to walk many more miles.

Thanks to Carter for literally walking miles with me in the park. Your trust in me has made me a better man.

Thanks to the two hundred-plus young men from the Men in the Bible class I taught over the years at Christ Presbyterian Academy. You were there through the early stages of this content. You know the surprising path to manhood.

Thanks to my daughters, Abigail and Rachel, for all their support.

Finally, thanks to Heidi for thirty-two years of being together. We both know the best is yet to come.

CONTENTS

I AM NO HERO

Men are incurably fascinated with the heroic.

They are mesmerized by heroic men they see in movies. They are pulled toward heroic tales they read in books. They are drawn to heroic deeds in the news. Some strange resonance is at work here, calling something out to a man—unbidden and unknown.

But the resonance doesn't last.

Back in the world of bosses and bills, tests and emails, it fades into the background—or into nonexistence. Perhaps it was a dream. Perhaps it was a silly notion. Perhaps it was nothing at all. Back in the world of the familiar, men feel something very different.

They feel uninitiated. Entering the work world, they have the bodies of men but inside they still feel like boys. Left without markers or guides to navigate the treacherous masculine terrain, they quickly become disoriented. To manage, they hunker down and latch onto anything for some sense of comfort or success.

They feel anonymous. Trying on different jobs and positions, they hope to land not just a steady income, but a clear-cut sense of identity. Yet it eludes them. They don't know who they are. And they don't know how to find it. They feel like shadows in the background.

They feel stuck. Stuck in work they tolerate or hate. Stuck in patterns that corrupt or imprison. If there was ever any sense of something burning inside of them to do, it has long been drowned out. The goal of life now is to survive. Some don't even do that.

If a man were to put words to all of this, it would come as a simple statement: "I am no hero." If you feel that way, join the rest of us.

Yet the resonance continues to call something out to us. Some mysterious voice bids us, *Come and follow. There is so much more to you. There is so much more to your life. You are meant for greater things. Come and follow, even if it costs you blood and spit, grime and grief—even if it costs you everything. In the end, you will lay your body down with no regrets. In the end, you will die a happy man.*

What is offered in this book is what it would look like to get up and follow that call. But I must issue a warning at the beginning. This path will be a surprise. The path we typically choose as men—well, that's what got us into trouble in the first place. True heroes are not necessarily the men who talk the loudest or seem the most successful. They are certainly not the ones who bully others into submission. Neither does the path lead to a stereotyped lumberjack or linebacker sort of manhood. Artists and athletes, musicians and hunters—whatever a man's gifts or proclivities, he is invited to take the same path. It is one that transcends typecast roles and cultural bounds.

That's why this way is different. That's why you must be ready for the unexpected. You must be prepared to enter the unknown. This is the surprising path into manhood.

Another warning. To get up and follow will change everything. It will turn everything upside down. The incalculable may happen. The impossible may be asked. Nothing will be the same as it was before.

One last thing to set the record straight: I am no hero either. Trust me on that one.

But I know Someone who is.

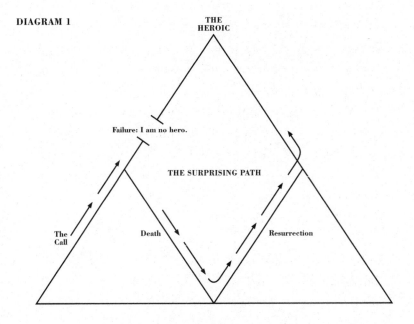

DIAGRAM 1

THE HEROIC

Failure: I am no hero.

THE SURPRISING PATH

The Call

Death

Resurrection

The ascent to the heroic requires a surprise turn
into death and resurrection. What that means
will be described in the pages ahead.

CHAPTER 1

SEARCHING FOR HEROES

"We are like sculptors, constantly carving out of others the image we long for, need, love or desire, often against reality, against their benefit, and always, in the end, a disappointment, because it does not fit them."
—Anais Nin

"The denigration of those we love always detaches us from them in some degree. Never touch your idols: the gilding will stick to your fingers."
—Gustave Flaubert, *Madame Bovary*

All flesh is as grass, and all the glory of man as the flower of the grass. The grass withers, and its flower falls away.
—1 Peter 1:24 NKJV

It's an ordinary family photo, yet if you look closer, it contains the contradiction of the ages.

It's a picture of me with my brother Tom. He is around four years old, making me about two. He had instigated the scene. I was just following suit, wanting to copy him. But it is our mother who had made the scene possible. She had taken two towels and wrapped one around each of our necks. Then she fastened them so that most of the towel became a cape, draping down our backs. My brother has a triumphant smile on his face, looking off in the distance with eyes that glow. My own eyes are transfixed on Tom. There we both are, ready to be Superman, ready to be "faster than a speeding bullet, more powerful than a locomotive, able to leap tall buildings in a single bound." Those words from the 1950s Superman TV show are still etched in my memory.

Tom had probably watched the show, becoming captivated by this visitor from another planet. Superman appeared to be a normal man in disguise, but he was more than a man. And he was more like the man Tom wanted to be. Of course at four years of age, he wasn't processing any of this consciously. But something about Superman had tugged at him enough that he wanted to dress up and fight "for truth, justice, and the American way." So did I.

On one level, this family photo is the standard fare of childhood behavior. From infancy, we learn by watching and copying, whether it's walking or talking, tying our shoes, or swinging a bat. Yet there is an additional element. Tom and I were not just learning a skill. We were copying a man we wanted to be like. But even here, there is nothing noteworthy. All boys look for a man to imitate, whether it's founded in reality with a grandpa or in the imaginary with those super-action figures.

But underneath these familiar terrains lies something else, as odd as it is common. It's a twist that should make us pause. On a purely rational level, the story of Superman is ridiculous. No man can bend steel or fly through the air. It's all right for young boys to imitate a mythologized character approaching the status of an ancient Greek god. But if a grown man attempts to be Superman, he is deemed psychotic. He has lost touch with reality. Yet no one wanted to spoil our boyhood imaginations that day, especially my mother, assuming that we would grow up and get in touch with reality.

So there we both were, standing triumphantly in our backyard with capes unfurled, dressed like thousands of other boys at that time, wanting to be what we could *never, ever become*. It is this contradiction that interests me. It is this twist that intrigues me. What was it about being more than a man, about being Superman, that captivated all of us boys? What was it about having superhuman strength and X-ray vision? About battling evil and rescuing the helpless? What was it about all this that so deeply resonated with those who had as yet no cognitive categories for such things? What is it about Superman that continues to captivate older audiences in all of the movie remakes? It is what we see in him, what we search for in others, and what we long to find in ourselves.

It is the heroic.

There is more to the Superman story. It's found in the life of the man who played Superman in the 1950s TV show, the actor George Reeves. Here is his story. After deciding to become an actor in high school, he got his first major break as one of Scarlett O'Hara's suitors in *Gone with the Wind*. But his real claim to fame came in landing the role of Superman in the TV series that ran from 1951–57. The series was scheduled to restart again in 1959, but it never happened. Instead, the police were called to his home and found George lying naked on his bed, bleeding where a bullet had shattered his temple and ripped through his brain. The newspapers reported that he had killed himself.

Rumors of George's struggle with alcoholism and depression certainly corroborated this story, but his mother was convinced that someone had murdered him. She attempted her own investigation using a private detective, but died before it was ever finished. George's girlfriend at the time disappeared right after his death, never to return, even for his funeral. She had been informed that he had left everything in his will to another lover, a married woman with whom he had had an affair for years, whose husband had connections to the criminal underworld.

Whether George committed suicide or was murdered by the mob, although an intriguing question, is not my point in retelling his story. It's the story itself. What did the life of George Reeves have to do with the life of Superman? Absolutely nothing. The contradiction is jarring. When I first heard his story, I was shocked and then saddened over his tragic life, cut short at forty-five years of age. I was also disappointed. Even though I knew that George was only acting as Superman, I had assumed something better than this sordid tale. In the end though, he was just another man struggling with his own set of sins and addictions—struggling and losing.

He was no Superman.

He was no hero.

THE SEARCH BEGINS

But we have jumped ahead of ourselves a bit. I want to return for a minute to the days of our boyhood heroes, to the time before disappointment and heartbreak. There is something here worth exploring and understanding. Think about it for a minute. Whom did you look up to as a boy? Whom did you admire as a young man? Who seemed to have the strength and skill to win the day? Who seemed to always know what to do and how to do it? Who fired your imagination with hopes of beating overwhelming odds? Who was your hero?

I began asking that question to a number of men. I heard so many different stories, but all with the same underlying passion as they spoke. Some of their heroes were celebrity figures. One of my faculty colleagues responded with Mickey Mantle, the Yankee baseball star who seemed to have it all. He could run, throw, hit, and field the ball—all with amazing skill. Following in the steps of icons Babe Ruth and Joe DiMaggio, he was treated like a hero, appearing on cereal boxes, baseball cards, and covers of national publications. My colleague loved baseball, so Mickey Mantle became his hero to admire. Another friend of mine, Jay, told the story of being drawn to a well-known SEC collegiate quarterback when he was a boy. Overcoming major injuries that should have ended his career, this quarterback refused to give up and fought his way back onto the playing field. It was his courage and tenacity that inspired Jay to keep playing football through his own setbacks and injuries—Jay eventually becoming an SEC quarterback himself.

Other heroes chosen were ordinary men whose impact was extraordinary. A former student of mine responded by naming his grandfather. When I asked him why, he looked straight at me without blinking and immediately replied: "He seemed invincible." Another friend, Tim, answered with the story of an older brother. Raised by parents who were distant and cold, this brother became the sole family connection for his heart. Tim played all the sports growing up, but his brother loved the outdoors instead. So they would spend hours bushwhacking through the expanse of woods bordering his house, camping out at night and talking about life. It is no surprise that Tim loves backpacking in the wilderness to this very day.

There are countless other hero stories I have heard: the rugby coach who instilled the value of hard work, the Scoutmaster who inspired so many to be Eagle Scouts, the older brother who sacrificed so much to join the army, the high school administrator who led by serving, and the teacher who inspired a student to become a novelist. I had a religion professor in college whose reputation was stellar. When I took his class, I saw why. He wasn't an exceptional lecturer or brilliant thinker. But on most afternoons you could find him in his office rocking chair, counseling students and encouraging them. I was one of those he listened to in that rocker. In fact, I was so taken with the man that I began to imitate him in my mannerisms and speech.

We love hearing stories like these because they stir up in us our highest aspirations, as well as the memories of our own heroes. Starting as young boys, we search for heroes, hoping to find and imitate them, so as to become heroic ourselves. But what exactly are we looking for in our heroes? What is it that gives them such magnetic power?

The most obvious trait of our early heroes is their physical strength and prowess. We are looking for the strong man. Often we choose athletes, for these men seem to possess the strength to beat the enemy and win the day. Who isn't inspired at times by the competitors we see in collegiate sports, the Tour de France, or the Olympic Games? And which of these great athletes didn't have someone inspiring them as a boy? Scott, another one of my friends, grew up with an older brother who possessed uncanny athletic ability. In whatever sport he took up—be it football, basketball, or lacrosse—he excelled. Along with the skill went a fighting spirit. He hated practices and just wanted to compete. When Scott entered the sixth grade, a time when school sports start to become important, he began to look up to his brother as a hero to imitate. I have heard similar stories end-lessly repeated by men who found their first hero in a strong man.

But there is more than just raw strength that pulls us to our heroes. During early manhood, we begin look-ing for someone who understands life and can point out the true path amid the jungle of lies. We are looking for the wise man. One of my students loved Captain Kirk of *Star Trek*, precisely because he used his wits and intellect rather than a display of power. It was the captain's wisdom that won the day. For me, I was mesmerized by the character of Yoda when *The Empire Strikes Back* appeared in theaters. I was intently searching then for someone who knew the truth and would train me in it. Yoda did just that when he helped Luke Skywalker understand the Force, training him in the ways of the Jedi.

But at some point, we are drawn to another type of hero, one who uses his strength and wisdom not for his own benefit but for others. We are looking for the noble man. Here is the quintessential hero, the one who lives for a transcendent purpose, not for his reputation. And he remains true to that purpose even when it costs him dearly. We are drawn to this warrior who fights for the good, precisely because he does it for everyone else. So many of the heroic men in story and film exhibit this prized quality. You only have to think of William Wallace, Maximus, Jean Valjean, or Aragorn to see the noble man in action. We feel a masculine energy pulsating from him, a fire in his soul that strikes something deep in ours. We want to burn as he does.

It's important to note several things here. First, I have used words like *pull, admire,* and *inspire* to delineate the power our heroes have over us. But these words don't quite have enough bite. Let me go at it this way. I recently read a newspaper article about a successful collegiate football coach on his first public appearance before the season. From young boys to elderly men, they all crammed into a hotel lobby for hours, waiting to get a brief glimpse or an autograph. Perhaps they might even get a chance to touch him. When he appeared, bedlam erupted as the crowd surged forward. Security guards tried to keep order as press cameras flashed incessantly. Shouts of, "We love you, coach," were heard over the commotion. It was all over quickly, but the hours of waiting seemed worth it for those who had gathered. The reporter suggested that these football fans saw their coach almost as a god-like figure. Then he gave a name to what he had seen. Hero worship. There it is—*worship*. That's the word I'm looking for. That's the power our heroes have on us. We put them up on a pedestal and worship them in wonder and adoration. Whether this is legitimate or questionable is another issue. My point is that we all do it, without premeditation or understanding why. It's inside all of us, the longing to idolize our chosen heroes.

The second thing to note is that no one sits us down as boys and teaches us about the heroic. No one explains to us the strength, wisdom, and noble character we should be looking for in our heroes. Even further, no one exhorts us to start searching for such men and follow their steps. We receive no instruction on this matter whatsoever. It is entirely innate, planted in some deep recess of our hearts. Long before we could even spell the word *hero*, we were already looking for one and looking up to one.

Finally, what is at the bottom of our search for the heroic? It is this: We are looking for the ideal man. We are looking for true masculinity. We know that we don't have it, and we know that we must find a hero to get it. But even further, we long to connect to that hero, hoping to warm ourselves in that masculine fire so as to ignite one in ourselves. It is this hope that sets us off on the trail—ever hunting, ever searching.

TROUBLES ON THE TRAIL

But somewhere along the way, the trail grows cold. The search becomes confusing. We awaken to troubling realities that disturb our grasp of the heroic. We awaken to death and evil, to sin and shame. We find that our heroes aren't the men we thought they were, the men we needed them to be.

All my life, I have longed for men to be more than what they could be, setting me up for the inevitable letdown. Often it came drip by drip, slowly dissolving my ideal image of them, as acid does to metal. One of my early heroes was a pastor known for his leadership ability and intellectual acumen. I loved standing in line to greet him after the service. The firm handshake would be followed by some banter between us. He would then throw his head back in laughter. In the joy he radiated, I sensed he had the fire I needed. But as I grew older, I learned of his inability to connect with others beyond the surface level. As far as I knew, he had few, if any, deep friends. What was he hiding that he didn't want others to see? My image of him eroded, and I became conflicted over how I should feel about him.

Other early heroes of mine included popular musicians. As a budding one myself, I was taken by their skill and creativity, as well as the aura they radiated on stage. One artist I was particularly drawn to was Dan

Fogelberg. There was something about his haunting melodies and poetic lyrics that captivated me. I learned most of the songs he ever wrote, performing them and copying his style in my own songs. But sometime later, I happened to meet someone who knew Dan personally. I was told troubling stories of relational wreckage and alcohol abuse. I left the conversation feeling confused. What was I to do with my tarnished image? I had no answer.

But at other times, the image didn't slowly erode. It shattered. By my sophomore year in college, I was drowning in a morass of doubt and despair about the big questions of life. As a result, I developed a keen interest in philosophy, expectant that it could give me the answers I desperately needed. Along with that interest, I was searching for a wise man. And I set my hope on a philosophy professor to fill that void. But my hopes were unraveled as the class proceeded. Instead of taking up the universal questions of God and reason, goodness and truth, I only remember petty discussions involving psychological conundrums (How do you describe green to a blind person?) and linguistic puzzles (Does a tree make a sound if it falls in the forest but no one hears it?).

But the real shattering happened as I came out after class one day and happened to see him conversing with another professor. They were strolling through the shade-filled lawn that separated the academic buildings. As I innocently walked behind them, I realized I could overhear their conversation. My professor was enthusiastically sharing his anticipation of an upcoming philosophy convention where he could party and drink. I was stunned. I had already seen my share of drunken bodies and reckless behavior. I had already walked through enough dorms the morning after, reeking of stale beer and vomit. Wherever goodness and truth were to be found, I knew it was not there. My wise man had shattered. The one I had looked to for rescue from drowning—hoping for a rope, a life preserver, anything—had just thrown me an anchor. I walked away staggering, drowning again.

My experiences are only repeated in some form with the other hero stories I have mentioned. Remember Scott's admiration for his athletic older brother? It turned to confusion and dismay as he got older. His brother became addicted to alcohol in college and then moved on to drugs, souring relationships in the family as he became more narcissistic. Scott realized that his brother was no longer someone to follow. He was someone from whom he had to distance himself. He did not want his life to turn out that way. What happened to Tim's older brother, to all of those moments they shared camping in the woods together? All that abruptly ended with his older brother's death in an accident, thrown from a car because he was not wearing a seat belt. At fourteen, Tim was devastated, left alone in a family unwilling and unable to grieve. What about the story of Mickey Mantle? It, too, crashed as a heroic tale. To numb the pain of his father's death from Hodgkin's disease (and figuring he would die from it as well), Mickey turned to alcohol, eventually destroying his marriage and estranging his family. My friend Jay who played collegiate football later find out that his own football hero had left a trail of relational devastation behind him through anger and manipulation. And what about that student of mine who believed that his grandfather was invincible? I asked him when he learned otherwise. He replied with three words: "My grandpa died."

The stories of our failed heroes come in all shapes and sizes, of uncles discovered with pornography, of cousins who sexually abused, of coaches caught lying, of athletes cheating with drugs, of teachers living secret lives, of musicians using the stage to hide—all once admired, all now defrocked. You have heard these stories yourself. You have known these men yourself.

The trail grows cold because the radiance we felt in our heroes fades. The fire flickers. Whether through their foolish choices or the specter of death, they cease to be the men we thought they were. We can no longer reach up to them. They have dropped down to us. What we do with our fallen heroes now becomes part of the continuing confusion. For some of us, we keep looking for a new hero to follow. For others, we try to shut down the longing, embracing worn-out platitudes: "People will let you down." "Don't trust others; you can only trust yourself." "Everyone makes mistakes." But I suspect for most of us, it's an odd combination of both routes. This is the energy behind the heightened expectations we feel for the new minister, the new CEO, or the newly elected politician. We need these men to be heroic leaders who can fight and come through for us. Yet when the inevitable disappointment comes, we scurry back into our self-protective corners, musing over our dreams broken once again. Worse still, we develop a cynicism that anticipates the dark side, congratulating ourselves when it appears: *We were right after all. Everyone has dirty laundry. Everyone has skeletons in the closet. There are no heroes. That's just a fairy tale.* But with such a settled conviction, the fire goes out. Suddenly we're in darkness.

A LIGHT IN THE DARKNESS

What are we to make of such contradiction and confusion? What are we to do with such dashed dreams and ideals? What do we do with our failed heroes? The Bible sheds some unique light in this darkness. A good place to begin is Paul's summary statement on the condition of humanity: "For all have sinned and fall short of the glory of God" (Rom. 3:23). Sin is described here as falling short—as lacking something or being destitute of something. But the most intriguing part of this statement is what we are lacking: the glory of God.

Glory is one of the more significant words in the Bible's vocabulary. When used of God, it denotes the luminous radiance with which He is surrounded whenever He reveals Himself. It's a radiance that leaves an unforgettable impression. The sense of impression probably comes from the Hebrew root behind *glory*, a verb that means to be heavy or weighty. God's glory is that. It's too heavy and weighty to be ignored. It etches a mark on all who experience it so that they are forever changed.

But there is more to glory than its definition. God's glory becomes thematic for the story of the Bible. Genesis 1 starts that story with God going to work as a skilled artisan. All of creation is endowed with a radiance that reflects the glory of the Creator. We see it in the purplish-hued sunsets, in the sweeping mountaintop vistas, and in the dome of the night sky that is jeweled with countless points of twinkling light. But more important, mankind was created in the likeness of that glory. We were to be godlike, sharing in that glory. We were to reflect it and bathe in it, enjoying Him and each other. This was to be our heritage and our life. But alas, we have lost the glory. The story of the fall in Genesis 3 is the story of all of us. Like our first parents, we believe the lie that true life is found outside of walking with God. We believe that He is, in fact, holding out on us and can't be trusted. So we choose to go and find life on our own. In so doing, we fall—we all fall short of the glory of God. We become destitute, stripped of that glory, not because He turns away from us but because we have turned away from Him and can no longer reflect that glory. Yet we do not cease to exist, but live in a kind of shadow world, where we only half exist. We are not men, but phantoms of our true selves. We have lost *our* glory, and the penalty is the very lack of glory itself. We are left hungering for it.

Perhaps you already see the connection with our search for heroes. Left in this shadow world, we are incurable hero-makers. We long for men to be more than what they are because they were *supposed* to be that way. The faint glimmers and isolated flashes of that original glory we sometimes see in men compel us to place them on a hero pedestal and worship them. We think, *Here is the answer to our search. Here is the true man.* Yet our worship becomes bitter idolatry. Disillusionment and heartbreak inevitably follow.

This is nowhere truer than in the masculine figure closest to us. To that one man we now turn.

THE FATHER EFFECT[1]

---

*"The plan from the beginning of time was that
his father would lay the foundation for a young
boy's heart and pass on to him that essential
knowledge and confidence in his strength."*
—John Eldredge, *Wild at Heart*

*"To be separated from a father hurts, no
matter how wounded or sinful he may have
been, and to reject ourselves in rejecting
him certainly compounds the pain."*
—Leanne Payne, *Crisis in Masculinity*

*Fathers, do not exasperate your children;
instead, bring them up in the training
and instruction of the Lord.*
—Ephesians 6:4

In all my years growing up, I have only one life-giving memory of my father.

I was in the fifth or sixth grade, and during that time, I experienced a recurrent fear about him. Whenever he was late coming home from work, I imagined that he had been killed in a car accident. The fear erupted one evening as I was sitting in the living room before dinner was to be served. I was talking to my grandmother, who was visiting at the time, and waiting on my father to come home. I could feel my anxiety building as the minutes ticked by. *When would he arrive? Had something terrible happened? What if he never came home?* I was explaining something to my grandmother to keep my mind occupied, something I had probably learned in school. As a part of the explanation, I remember taking my two hands and holding them out in front of me, touching them and then tracing a diagonal line down with one of the hands. Just at that moment, I heard the unmistakable sound of my father's Porsche zooming up the driveway. I felt a surge of joy run up through me. I hastily finished the explanation to my grandmother and ran into the kitchen to greet him as he came up the basement steps. He was tired and worn from the day—but he was home. The casual greeting between us communicated nothing of significance. Yet for me, it was life. I could see his face. He could see mine. That was all I needed.

Even if this story can be written off as classic separation anxiety, it is still a precious memory to me. It is the one time I felt joy in my father's presence—such a contrast to what I usually felt.

My father was a conscientious, hardworking doctor at a time when doctors were expected to put in long hours—even over weekends. When he did come home, he would retreat to his office after dinner to keep the family finances and prepare for the next day. As a result, I have no memory of my father ever wrestling with my brother or me, reading to us at night, tucking us into bed, or telling us stories of his past. There are few memories I have of him doing anything with me. And even those memories carry a lingering sense of anxiety that he felt, anxiety that could erupt into anger when provoked. So I learned from an early age to steer clear as much as I could.

Out of this experience with my father, I intuited an idea that was to become bedrock truth for years: *I am on my own. There is no one to help me. This is the way life is.* The idea of asking for help or instruction rarely occurred—and then only in crisis. So much of my sadness and loneliness in high school came from such wholesale disconnection. By that time, though, the disconnection from my father had grown into disgust. I hated him and wanted out of his life. That wish came true one late summer morning as I set off for college in my red Toyota Celica jammed with books, clothes, and other personal belongings. By the time I had driven down to the bottom of our driveway, I was already congratulating myself on being able to leave him forever. I was hoping never to return.

I have listened to so many men, young and old, tell stories of the same order, different in detail but universal in devastation. There were fathers who left for other women, fathers who left for other men, fathers entangled in alcoholism or sexual addiction, fathers whose criticism was a constant sandpaper, fathers whose silence cut like a cold scalpel, fathers who gave up and committed suicide, fathers whose shaming words became defining, fathers whose behavior shamed their sons.

You have heard these stories. You may have lived one of these stories.

OUR FIRST HEROES

But this is not the way it was meant to be. Our fathers were supposed to be the primary conduits of masculinity, giving us something of their noble hearts. In the way God set up creation, they were to be our first heroes, striking the masculine fire in us. How were they to do that? By word and deed.

The word is the blessing of verbal affirmation. Every boy needs to feel settled inside of himself. He needs to feel okay in his skin. That interior assurance comes best by the affirming word of the father. This is the only way a boy can separate from his mother and enter the landscape of masculinity. The affirmation can come from something as simple as a morning high-five. It can come from a compliment about a good play in the soccer game or a good grade on a spelling test. It can happen when the father notices the son being a good friend or a good leader. It can happen when the son has shown resolve in the face of pressure or courage in the face of fear. But if the affirmation only focuses on behavior or accomplishment, the son can imagine that it comes by his performance. This thinking lays the groundwork for the pressure many sons feel to keep accomplishing, fearing that failure will mean a loss of affirmation—and with that a loss of masculine connection.

But notice the difference in these two statements: "That was a great catch you made in the game today." "I'm so glad you're my son." One deals with accomplishment. The other relationship. However much a boy needs to be encouraged about his performance, that is not the center of his heart. The center lies in how the father feels about him. When the affirmation is directed here, the son will feel the warmth of the fire and catch it himself. He will glow. I am not speaking in metaphor.

Recently, I attended the birthday party of a thirteen-year-old son, whose father wanted this day to be a benchmark, crossing his son into manhood. He gathered me and ten other men for a sumptuous dinner in a private room of a well-known Italian restaurant. Our meal was to be followed by offering whatever wisdom we could to the son. At first, he felt anxious, surrounded by so many men, all there to speak to him. But something shifted inside him as the men each stood to speak, starting and ending with his father. They all conveyed something important to remember as he entered manhood. They also offered verbal affirmation. They told stories of his loyalty as a friend, his standing up to bullying, his love for his sisters, and his courage and goodwill. As the evening progressed, I kept noting the son's face. It glowed—literally. He was basking in the fire and reflecting it. It was an evening he will never forget.

But along with the verbal affirmation, something else is needed—the deed, the active engagement. Here the father comes alongside to be present in the son's life, to play and to coach. It could be pretending to be superheroes in the bedroom with toy weapons. It could be lessons in hooking a worm so they can fish off a dock. It could be setting up the tent for a night under the stars in the backyard. It could be showing how to change a car tire on the side of the road. It could be throwing the ball or tying the knot or shooting the pistol. The activity doesn't matter. The engagement does.

When a father chooses to play with his son and offer whatever skill he has, something is transmitted that can only come this way—the otherliness of masculinity. This otherliness is why fathers feel so heroic to boys. They are born with the distant echo of man's untainted glory planted inside. But it is still latent and inaccessible to the son. The father becomes the primary way that sleeping memory is resurrected. The boy sees his dad in resonant color and feels masculinity strike inside of him. He awakens and longs to follow.

A friend relayed the story of watching a pickup truck filled with jams and produce pull into the parking lot of a small country town. A man in his thirties stepped out and came around to the other side to let out his business partner—a son about five years old. As they set everything up to be sold out of the bed of the pickup, you could see the active engagement. The father was gently coaching the young boy in basic politeness to customers: "Make sure you say, 'Thank you,' and, 'Yes, ma'am.'" You could also hear the verbal affirmation: "Good job placing those jams out, Bubba. Way to go!" When my friend asked the father if Bubba was the son's real name, he got this response: "No. That's not his real name, but I call him Bubba when it's just us guys around." With that kind of intentionality, the father was already leading his boy into the terrain of masculinity. The son felt so confident in the dad's coaching that when the set-up was completed, he got behind the wooden stand to be lead seller. He was ready for business.

Bob, one of my close friends, was also intentional about bringing his son into masculine territory by taking him duck hunting from an early age. The son grew up learning to manage a cold shotgun behind blinds that overlooked fields flooded with icy waters. He was coached and felt at home in the world of hunting: the predawn waiting, the expectant whispers, the sharp crack of the gun, and the plummet of a slain duck. But he also felt at home with his father. One evening, Heidi and I were invited over to dinner with their family. Now a young man, I watched with surprise as the son plopped himself down in his father's lap for a moment after dinner. Such physical closeness was not only acceptable but normal.

VIOLENT AND SILENT

Sadly, these stories of affirmation and engagement are rare. For every one of them, I have heard countless others that move in the opposite direction. Here the fathers cannot strike in their sons any sense of masculinity. They do not awaken the latent memory of a hero. They do not stoke the fire. Instead, they snuff out the tiny blaze struggling to survive. Or they are frozen and have no fire to give. They are the violent and silent fathers.

The violent father is engaged, but in a way that wounds rather than affirms. He can be physically or emotionally abusive, and the abuse can be overt or deadly subtle. Ed had a stellar high school soccer career. After giving all that he had and playing the game of his life, scoring three goals and an assist, his father came up to him for the usual post-game commentary. Ed hoped that he would finally be pleased with such a performance. His father did offer a brief note of congratulations, but then proceeded to scold him for his inconsistencies defensively, dressing him down for his flaws and mistakes. Ed was shattered. Nothing was ever good enough for his father. Nothing would ever make him happy.

John tells the story of playing chess with his father as a boy. It was one of the things they did together. He knew enough to play the game, but not enough to compete. He remembers one particular series of chess games that all ended the same way—it was checkmate for John. The father kept beating him again and again and again until he was in tears. There was not one word of instruction or encouragement from the dad during the whole ordeal. It was his mother who finally stopped the bloodletting: "Oh, let him win." For John's father everything in life was a competition, one that he had to win, even if it was just chess with his young son. It took years for John to realize that he didn't have to compete with every man in his life. He could even trust some of them.

Daniel's story begins with parents who already had four sons. Hoping for a daughter with their fifth pregnancy, she was tragically stillborn. They decided to try one more time even though they were getting on in years. The pregnancy was difficult and required the mom to be put on bed rest, but that only increased their anticipation. After Daniel was born, the father pulled back the sheets in the hospital crib, saw his fifth son, and cursed. Then he turned and walked out. Being an unexpected boy, he had no name, so those at the hospital gathered to put names down on slips of paper and put them in a wallet. The name Daniel was drawn out, and that became his. The angry cursing and random naming that began his life cast a dark shadow that followed him in a home where he wasn't desired. It came out especially in the impatience his father expressed with him. As a part-time repairman, the father toted him around as a boy, so he wouldn't be left by himself at home. When asked to get a certain tool but having no instruction on the matter, he would often come back with the wrong one. When asked to hold the flashlight, he would get distracted and drop the beam. Both violations received reprimands and more cursing. It has taken years for Daniel to voice his story of abuse and even more years to begin to heal.

When a son grows up with a violent father, there is no glow. There is no glory. There is a trail of devastation left running through his heart. But the silent father is just as destructive, maybe more so. Instead of engagement or affirmation, there is nothing at all. No voice. No presence. No touch. The silence is deafening. The father has no fire to give, and the son is left abandoned out in the cold to shiver.

Mike is a colleague of mine who grew up with a silent father. The silence came through a lack of presence. His dad was an outgoing man who loved to hunt, fish, golf, and play poker with the guys on Tuesday nights. He never once invited his son into any of these activities, even when he became a young man. It's been years since his father died in a tragic accident, yet he still longs to feel close to him.

My friend David came from a home riddled with conflict between parents. There was always a lingering tenseness in the air, compounded by a father with a drinking problem who kept threatening to leave. One day in the seventh grade, he came home to a stillness that was eerie. When his dad didn't come home at the expected hour, he asked his mom, "Where's Daddy? I want to see him. I want to talk to him." Even after repeated attempts to understand where his father was, the only response the mom would give was that she didn't know. He remembers vividly the loneliness, the stomachaches, the silence, the anxiety: *Where is Dad? What has happened to him?* After two long weeks, his mother finally told him that his father had left home. The threat had become reality. No other explanation was given. For another two miserable years, he went back and forth between his parents' homes, feeling trapped in the middle, until his dad died of a stroke. He tried to bury the pain of abandonment by becoming a champion athlete and honor student. Instead, it turned out to be the beginning of his long battle with depression.

Frank tells the story of a silent father who worked in the HVAC business. As a boy, he went to the workshop one Saturday with his father to pick up some ornamental metal work. As they walked in, the father received a phone call from his own father. With a warning to leave the machines alone, his father went into the office to take the call. As a curious eleven-year old, he soon forgot his father's warning and began looking at the machines, especially one with shiny rollers and pedals. It was a machine that cut sheet metal. In one nightmarish moment, he decided to push down the foot pedals as his hands were on the rollers, only to find his fingers on both hands caught up and smashed in the rollers. In the bloody chaos and surgery that followed, he lost several of his fingers. During the recovery from his trauma, he had to be tutored at home with his schoolwork. His life was changed forever, but his father never spoke one word about it to him. No conversation, no sympathy, no sorrow, no encouragement—nothing, just silence. To add to the misery of his situation, his extended family at their weekly dinners labeled him as stupid for doing something so foolish. No wonder that when he came of age as a young man, he turned to drugs to silence the pain. His mangled hand reflected a deeper wound—a mangled heart.

THE FALLOUT

Look around you. The effect of violent and silent fathers is everywhere. The fallout is in the air we breathe. It's in the tragic headlines of the newspapers. It's in the shocking stories on the TV news. It's in the endless statistics of men who inflict trauma. But in the heart of the son, the fallout strikes at his core—his identity.

For the son of a violent father, what he hears becomes who he is. The son who is told he is never good enough finds some way to keep failing. The son who is labeled a coward continues to cringe in fear. The son who is called stupid gives up on school. What a father says about him feels like a prison sentence for life, so he ends up living out those expectations. With the silent father, the son feels alone. He is on his own to figure life out and has to make the best of it. Asking for help is not even considered. This accounts for the isolation so many men feel, one that slowly cripples them.

In both types of sons, the longing to find a hero in the father has long been buried. The fragile hope has been smashed. There is no noble man here. There never was. And with that longing buried comes a savage disconnect from the masculine structure of the world. It's as if an umbilical cord has been yanked out of a son's soul. He is left bleeding, convulsing, struggling to breathe.

In that struggle to survive, the son will turn any-where to find something that feels masculine. It could be the reckless behavior of peers, even if it's self-destructive. It could be playing the tough, angry guy that keeps everyone at bay. It could be turning to a woman and demanding that she make him feel like a man. It could be homosexual pursuits hoping to scavenge for his mas-culinity by sexual means. But none of this will lead him to the ancient dream of the hero. None of this will make him noble. It will only ruin him.

But the worst fallout may lie in how a son now feels about God. Fathers were meant to be a son's first taste of God the Father. As such, fathers become the emotional template for a son's own connection with God. The engaging, affirming father paves a clear path into the father-love of God. But sons of violent fathers often feel God to be condemning, and they have difficulty trust-ing Him. Having known violation from their dads, their instinctive motion is to defend and self-protect—and for good reason. But trust requires an open heart, something that feels uncomfortable or even impossible for them. For the son of a silent father, God appears distant. He may believe that God loves the world, but only in a generic sense. Feeling loved personally is not a part of his soul's structure. God may be there, but not there for him. These felt categories about God become part of the matrix of how the son sees the world, whatever formal theology he may hold in his mind. His functional beliefs, residing in his gut, are what truly define him.

RUNNING AWAY

But there is still one more part of the fallout to consider. Every son longs for his dad to be a hero. Every son needs his dad to be a hero. But for so many sons, their fathers became anti-heroes from whom they run away. This explains the vow so many men carry *never* to be like their fathers. But running away is not the answer. It only complicates everything. I know from personal experience.

After college, I spent the next season of my life as a married man and father of two, trying desperately *not* to be like my father. I was determined not to repeat his silence. But it all came crashing down in an argument I had one day with Heidi. We were in the bedroom locked in a disagreement over something I have long since forgotten. Standing on opposite sides of the bed, the argument escalated. Expressing her justifiable frustration with me, she hurled these words, "You are just like your father." I felt as if I had been stabbed by a dagger. I collapsed onto the bench at the foot of the bed. She was right. Somehow, despite my best efforts, I had been repeating my own father's workaholic lifestyle and disconnection, the one I had hated. I, too, had become a workaholic. I had become obsessed with my growing success as a teacher and coach, spending hours on the job during the day and working hard at night to prepare for the next day. What little attention I paid to Heidi felt to her as if she were an interruption in my list of pressing tasks. I was left in massive upheaval. So many of the heroes I had tried to imitate had disappointed me. Now on top of that, I had become like the one man I had intentionally tried *not* to imitate. What was I to do with the mess I had made of my life? Who could straighten this wretched tangle?

I have to say here that my father is not an evil man, but someone with his own set of endearing qualities and character flaws. Having long since reconciled with him and now understanding some of his own story, I know that he was caught in his own set of entanglements. He was trying to do the best that he could and failing along the way. He, too, was the product of a silent father and was just passing on what he had been given. I have grown to love him in his later years, but I now know that he could never give what I so terribly needed during my formative years.

The Scriptures lend credence to the power of fathers in a remarkable verse that closes the Old Testament. It is a prophesy of the Messiah and the redemption He will inaugurate. How will He stop the spread of sin's curse? How will He make everything right again? Here's how: "And he will turn the hearts of fathers to their children and the hearts of children to their fathers, lest I come and strike the land with a decree of utter destruction" (Mal. 4:6 ESV). He will stop fathers and sons from running away from each other and start turning their hearts toward each other. This is the undoing of the curse. But when that healing work is refused, the destruction continues.

Yet I see that healing work in the good fathers I know who have turned their hearts toward their sons. The fire is being lit. The glory is being caught. On a camping trip with some fathers and sons, I pulled one of the boys aside and told him I thought he had hit the lottery when it came to fathers. He responded by looking at me with eyes shining with love for his father. He didn't have to say anything. I could see the glow. I had watched his father constantly engage and affirm him on the trip. The son felt so safe in his father's love. Despite the fact that we were in the middle of the untamed Colorado wilderness over ten thousand feet in elevation, he feared no danger with his father nearby. Come bears or storms or snow, it didn't matter. All was well with his father there.

I think the greatest compliment a son could ever give his father is this: "You are my hero." The father has loved his son well, and the son has received that love well. The turning has begun. But even the best of fathers is still a sinner. Even the greatest of dads falls short of the glory of God. The heroic gleam is dim at best. The son may warm himself in that fire for a while, but at some point, he will have to navigate his own way forward in a world where confusion and disappointment seem to have the upper hand. The father cannot protect his son from all evil, much less the evil in the son's own soul.

Sadly, this confusion and disappointment only escalates when the son attempts to be a hero himself. But that takes us to the next chapter.

CHAPTER 3

CHASING FALSE GLORY

"Our greatest fear should not be of failure but of
succeeding at things in life that don't really matter."
—Francis Chan, *Crazy Love*

"I think everybody should get rich and famous
and do everything they ever dreamed of so
they can see that it's not the answer."
—Jim Carrey tweet

"This is what the LORD says, 'I will overthrow
what I have built and uproot what I have planted,
throughout the earth. Should you then seek
great things for yourself? Do not seek them.'"
—Jeremiah 45:4–5

I have always wanted to be famous. And even though I know that many famous people live miserable lives, that never made the longing go away.

It first erupted during my college years in an attempt to make it as a songwriter. My Yamaha six-string became a constant companion as I labored to create original chord progressions with a melody and lyrics to match. I amassed pages of songs, in the hope of recording them and going to the next level. That hope became reality when a friend with home studio equipment saw their potential. We spent one entire summer recording a set of them, often working late into the night. When the set of ten songs was completed, he took them to a well-known producer to mix the tracks. I was thrilled with the result. This was going to be my ticket into musical stardom. I sent the finished demo to a number of music industry execs, hoping for a green light from someone. Instead, I got silence or rejection. In the anguish of my disappointment, I gave up. My dream to become a famous musician had hit a dead end.

Then through a strange series of events, I decided to enter the ministry and, in time, became a church planter. Like any young pastor on such a venture, I had images of what I hoped the church would become, but the images all tended to center on me. I daydreamed about preaching before hundreds, even thousands, of eager listeners, hanging on my words. All would hear me and be in awe. I told myself I was doing this for God, and I sincerely wanted to. But was I? Unfortunately, my attempt at fame here turned out no better than the first. After four years of plowing away at it, I became drained and depressed, unable to take on the daily tasks of life. To survive, I stepped down as the pastor. Soon after I left, the young church shut its doors forever. Another dead end.

Then, through an even stranger series of events, a door opened for me to teach and coach at a Christian high school. It all seemed to be coming together. Students petitioned to be in my Bible classes. Young men flocked to my cross country and track programs.

Administrators and parents loved what I was doing. I had finally found some measure of fame and thought that contentment would soon follow. But that's not what happened. Instead, I felt jealous of teachers or coaches who experienced any measure of success. They were encroaching on my territory and taking me out of the spotlight. So I felt driven to keep pushing to be the best. With that came an ever-mounting pressure to perform at the high standards I had set for myself. Each class I had to show my students I was the best teacher around. Each practice I had to prove to my athletes that I was the best coach imaginable. Along with the pressure came a low-grade anxiety I lived with every day. I felt on stage or always on call. As I mentioned in the last chapter, the pressure began to erode my marriage, but it also began to erode me with the stress and tension. I had found fame all right, but I never expected it to feel this way.

The confusion this created was wrenching. I felt chained to a longing that always led me to a dead end or to mounting pressure. What was I to do with a desire that never went away and continually deceived me? If I tried to push it down or ignore it, it would pop back up in another context. If I tried to follow it, it led to frustration and confusion. Only years later would I understand that my story is universal. Every man chases after a greatness that eludes him.

Take, for instance, the story of Ignatius, the founder of the Jesuits. His early years were framed by an incessant search for fame. He dreamed of being the noble warrior who would win the hearts of women by his daring deeds. As such, he trained to be a soldier in the army and a courtier to royalty. He was obsessed with his appearance and made a big show of walking about with his armor on, adding long hair and a bright cap to the swagger. He wanted to be noticed as the great man who would achieve great deeds. Of course, this type of posturing led to a proud disdain for other men touting their swagger. This may be the explanation behind a nighttime brawl for which Ignatius seemed responsible. As one Jesuit historian noted, he may be the only canonized saint with a notarized police record.

When I first read the story of Ignatius, I immediately connected with him. Remove the medieval trappings, and his longing was mine. In his own words, it was "a great and foolish desire to win fame." And like my story, his search landed him in a very unexpected place. After fighting in a battle, where he perhaps dreamed of heroic feats, he was struck by a cannonball, shattering his leg and forcing him to recuperate at his family castle. He then submitted to several painful operations, hoping that his leg would look attractive again in the tights of that day. Instead, he ended up with a limp the rest of his life. Rather than greatness and fame, Ignatius found disappointment and failure.

Ignatius's story is in some way the story of every man. What are we to do with a longing that always leads us astray? Let's first put some clearer language to it. On the surface, the longing seems to be connected to success. Every man desires success because it seems to offer him affirmation and fame before others. But there is more behind the desire for success. We also want to be known as men who have attained some level of greatness. And we want to feel that greatness inside of us. Perhaps you can see the longing now for what it is.

We want to be heroic.

Stated this way, the parallels with our previous search for heroes are revealing. Just like the search, our attempt to be a hero is never something we are taught. We take on the task unconsciously, driven on despite any prior instruction on the matter. Further, we are now attempting to become the men we once admired in our heroes. We hope by our efforts to acquire the strength and cunning they possessed. We want that same masculine fire burning within by which we warmed ourselves in their company.

Finally, we want that same admiration our heroes had from us. We once put them on a pedestal. Now we hoist ourselves up on that same pedestal, hoping others will look with awe and worship. This sounds scandalous, but I can think of nothing better to call it. The desire to have thousands listen to my preaching and be in awe of me—what else can I call that except worship? My attempt to lead others to God somehow always bent back around to me. Underneath my sincere religious wish lay a wild desire for heroic stature that spurned all efforts to be tamed.

A HOST OF OPTIONS

But the drive to be the hero of our stories can get reenacted in many other ways besides the pursuit of fame. The world pitches in and helps, offering a host of options. They call out to us with siren voices, all promising the strength and wisdom we seek. We hear them and blindly follow, unaware of what we will reap.

One of the most obvious options is athletic prowess. So many of our boyhood heroes had this trait, so it seems perfectly natural to chase after it. One of my running partners relayed this story to me during a training run. He was raised in Florida and attended a large public school known for its football program. At the beginning of his freshman season, his freshman teammates committed to the dream of attaining the ultimate prize, the state championship. For the next four years, they endured the brutal Florida heat, the incessant conditioning and weight lifting, and the sacrifice of time to achieve their goal. The dream became reality their senior year. They won the state championship. Ecstatic celebration ensued after the game that night. The next morning he awoke to find his picture on the front page of the sports section. But instead of celebrating, he felt empty. Out of that emptiness popped an unexpected question: *Is this all there is? Is this all it means to win?* He had no answer, only a sense that something terrible was amiss. Why didn't the championship deliver what it seemed to promise? Why didn't his athletic success translate into something solid in his heart?

While he was telling me this story, we were training together for a marathon. It was my own attempt at athletic achievement. Much later than he, I awoke to the same desire. I had always felt scrawny during high school, comparing my small frame to the muscular football players. Taking on a physical challenge like the marathon would be the answer. So I spent four months in training, taking on progressively longer runs in a park and then adding intervals around a local track. My life was consumed with training, eating, and sleeping. When the morning of the marathon arrived, I felt nervous yet confident I could pull it off. I caught sight of my cheering family at the eight-mile mark, signaling to them that I was feeling good by putting both thumbs up. Somewhere around the fifteen-mile mark though, it became harder to keep my pace. Unknowingly, I was succumbing to dehydration, something that dogged my steps over the rest of the marathon. I willed myself through the last mile and over the finish line, pale and disoriented. Heidi walked me to the first-aid tent where I downed two liters of fluid to recover. Yet the suffering had made the achievement sweeter. I had done it. I had finished a marathon. A few days later, though, I noticed old insecurities reappearing. I didn't feel any stronger inside. It left me with more questions: *Why didn't this work? Should I run another marathon? Where else do I need to turn to find strength?* There is nothing wrong with pushing oneself physically, and there are certainly benefits in the challenge. But now I know that such an endeavor doesn't translate into the interior landscape of a man. A muscular body does not equal a muscular soul.

There are many other options out there besides athletic endeavor, each promising a sure route to heroic status. Another common one is career success. Here a man fights his way up the ladder, proving his strength and skill. Call it ambition, call it drive, call it initiative, call it whatever you want—a man wants motion in his career, and it's always upward.

Sam tells the classic story of attempting to be the hero in his workplace. He got involved in the business side of medicine early in his career, buying up several small clinics and selling them. Then with five partners, he started a new company of clinics that became a sprawling enterprise, successful by anyone's metrics. He also got a doctorate along the way, convinced it would open up another platform of teaching at the college level. During the climb up, he longed to be known as the mover and shaker of his world, as the man who ran the show. He constantly looked for the next challenge to conquer, the next venture to make his mark. It also created in him an obsession with being right in the daily decisions of the business. But in the scramble to the top, he began to stop and watch blue-collar workers doing landscape work. On other occasions when he left late-night meetings, he saw those who cleaned the buildings and noticed how content they seemed to be. He wondered what it would be like to rid himself of the upward drive that had now become burdensome. He got his chance when the business was bought out. Now he could retire and relax. Soon into the retirement though, he learned that it was no nirvana. He was left with a host of questions. What kind of story had he written for himself? What kind of greatness had he achieved? And what was he looking for all of those years? His story could be repeated in the countless tales of career climbs and disappointments at the top.

Another path into heroic status seems to be offered with marriage. Every woman wants a prince in shining armor. The fairy tale is no illusion, but says something true about a woman's heart. She really is looking for a hero. Match that with our desire to be one, and it should lead to marital bliss. But that's not what happens. In every marriage, disappointments and conflicts emerge. If left untended, they can grow into anger and betrayal. The heroic tale we once believed becomes blurred to the point of non-recognition.

Dave tells the story of marrying a woman with a determination to show her that he was the man with the answers. He would also provide for her and never be unfaithful. As laudable as those goals were, they were based on a commitment formed from shaming boyhood experiences. He would never again appear foolish in front of others. It drove him to become the man who knew how to get things done. This determination translated into long hours at the workplace with little to give at home. When his wife began to express her deep loneliness and ask for more of him, he responded with resistance, thinking, *You've got a pretty good catch with me. You need to appreciate all I've done for you instead of whining and complaining.* Their marriage continued to drift over time, finally ending in divorce.

Other options for becoming the hero of our stories come at us from all angles. Some men pursue wealth and the power it gives. Some are hypnotized by social media, hoping to feel important with an increased following. Others chase reputation and the intoxication of being respected. Still others are driven by the idea of leaving their name imprinted on their accomplishments. But there are darker courses a man may choose.

GOING UNDERGROUND

If a man is dogged with failure and rejection in his attempt to find heroic greatness, the longing won't fade. It will just go underground, chasing after something to quell the pain. Whatever he finds for comfort will now become an attachment. This is the underlying energy behind the massive struggle so many men have with pornography.

Stan tells the story of feeling small and unassuming in high school. He felt painfully average in academics and athletics and struggled with hurtful comments by girls toward him. To make up for this lack of affirmation, he sought to become the nicest person at school, trying to please everyone along the way. Here he found success and won the senior superlative for the friendliest. But the commitment to please became exhausting. He needed a place to feel safe without having to perform. That place became pornography. The images became a drug to escape the pressure of trying to make everyone happy. The addiction that started in high school continued into college and beyond, even into his career as a Christian college professor. To manage the stress of performing, porn became a regular part of his life. It was his anesthetic. Only after he saw the damage it was causing his marriage did he decide to seek help.

Besides pornography, there are a host of other attachments men chase after for comfort—the next affair, the next workout, the next vacation, the next casino trip, the next dinner out. They vary in terms of social respectability, yet the energy behind them is the same. In preparing to write this book, I taught much of the material to a night class of men, some of whom came from halfway houses. Here, they were learning to piece their lives back together after having them shattered by drugs and alcohol. I got the chance to listen to their heartbreaking stories, often involving abandonment and abuse. I saw why they chose substance abuse. With the constant disappointment and betrayal from men in their lives, they went to a comfort readily available—liquor, marijuana, heroin, or often some combination. The comfort became an addiction. The addiction became a nightmare.

Finally, there are those who choose a more radical route to stop the pain. One of the young men who attended that same night class seemed especially quiet and attentive. After coming twice, I didn't see him again for several weeks. I soon learned why. His story involved an abusive, alcoholic father. One Christmas as a boy, he was taken into the coat closet and repeatedly slapped for no apparent reason. On another occasion after a poor performance on the golf course, he was pulled by the hair and thrown onto the green. He was told that he was never good enough and would never amount to anything. The trauma of his upbringing brought on bipolar depression, uncontrollable anger, and drug addiction. Even after rehab, he kept searching for the next event or the next possession that would ease the pain. What broke him was seeing his own raging anger with his girlfriend and realizing that he was becoming like his father. He couldn't face that prospect, so he took the deadliest combination of drugs possible to ensure that he would not be a failure here. The shock of his suicide rattled me and the class. I tell his story as a small way to honor his struggle. I also tell it as an example of how desperate our stories can become. When a man can't find any way to feel strong, any way to find affirmation, the pain can be so searing that death feels like a release.

THE MESS GETS MESSIER

If our search for heroes lands us in confusion, our attempt to be one only makes the mess messier. Nothing turns out as we thought. It's a reverse-Midas touch. Nothing turns to gold. Everything we touch spoils. What has happened to our hope of achieving heroic greatness? How did we create such a mess? The answer lies in a prior spoiling. There is a subtle but unmistakable shift that occurs when we pursue what we saw in our heroes. The strength we admired was their ability to overcome the odds and conquer the enemy. The wisdom we loved was their understanding of life and the skill to live it well. But in the attempt to interiorize both qualities, we corrupt them. Pushed through the filter of our destitute souls, they come out on the other side as something quite different: a grasping for fame, a chasing after success, or a grabbing at power. If the chase becomes a repeated failure, it reshapes itself into an addictive flight from the pain.

Other collateral damage comes with the corruption. In our attempted rise to heroic status, we become keenly aware of other men doing the same thing. My pastor friend calls it "compare and compete." He has shared with me on numerous occasions his struggle of comparing himself with other ministers and competing for bigger congregations. He will speak about feeling insecure over the savvy website another nearby church has set up. Then he will confess his pride rearing up as irritation at the posturing of other pastors. This seesaw battle is in every man's heart. Whether it's playing racquetball, starting a business, finding a trophy wife, or driving a sports car, the compare-and-compete war is fought on endless battlefields.

Along with this tug is a constant need to prove ourselves as men. Whatever success or fame we attain never produces a settled sense of greatness. The result? We start running on a treadmill with no stop button. Each success only starts a new cycle to prove we can do it again. Each achievement only sets up a new one after which we must chase. Yet if our attempts at heroic status really did work, shouldn't there be some place of attainment? If what we accomplished made us into the men we admired, shouldn't we feel it? But ignoring these questions, we keep running, assuming this must be the way.

Underneath the comparing and the proving is something more crippling—the cover-up. Most of us have had the nightmare of showing up at school or work only to see others laughing at us. We look down and discover to our horror that we have on underwear, or perhaps nothing at all. It's the universal fear in every man—to be caught naked and exposed. Out of that dread comes a preoccupation with covering our nakedness. Deep down, we know we are not strong, but weak and fearful. We know we are not wise, but confused and unsure.

So we grab at anything that feels like clothes, whatever will offer us some measure of approval as a man. The clothes then become necessary, as necessary as our routine of getting dressed. The thought of not having them rouses terror. What has happened here? We wanted to feel the fire inside of us that we felt in our heroes. We wanted to burn as they did. But instead of burning, we feel divided, split into the men we pretend to be and the men we really are. To keep the pretense, we must expend increasing amounts of energy. The effort becomes exhausting.

There is one last tangle to sort out the mess. Remember our ideal hero? He was the strong and wise man who used his strength and skill for the sake of others. He was the noble man we loved. But where is that noble man now? Instead of moving toward that ideal, we have backtracked. The drive to compare, to prove ourselves, and to cover up has not turned us into noble men. It has made us into narcissists. We seem incurably bent on warping reality to meet the demands of our desolate souls. We are not heroes, offering life to those around us. We are black holes, sucking life out of them.

In Greek mythology, Narcissus was one of the most beautiful young men anyone had ever seen, but he could never return the love of others. Instead, he saw a reflection of himself in a river and was so absorbed by it that he couldn't leave. He eventually perished beside the water, alone and unloved. The myth speaks to the universal pull inside every man to become self-absorbed, unwilling and then unable to see anyone but himself. He can't be heroic for others. He's too busy proving it to himself. The end of such a life is contemptible. One of the surest routes to evil is paved with narcissism. Once we lose the ability to empathize, once we become hopelessly entangled in the web of our own neediness, evil becomes potential—and then real. I do not speak in the hypothetical. I have watched too many narcissistic leaders grab at power by degrading others. I have watched too many narcissistic pastors inflict damage on those under their care. I have watched too many narcissistic husbands shred their wives. And I have had to watch Heidi deal with the wounds that came from my own narcissism.

SORTING THE MESS OUT

In the attempt to become heroic, we make a damned mess of our lives. I don't mean this as frivolous swearing. It's sober truth. The mess we make is damnable and will be judged as such. Where are we to go? How do we reverse this slide into oblivion?

We must go back to the beginning as we did in the first chapter. There we explored the idea of God's glory, the radiance of His revealed being, marking those who experience it. We can sense that glory in the created order, but we were meant to feel it in ourselves. God desired to share His glory with us so that we could feel our weight as men, clothed in that glory. But with the fall, we turned away, leaving us naked and cold. The surest thing we know about ourselves as men is that we lack something. That lack causes our pervasive shame. As the first fallen emotion of Adam, it becomes foundational for the framework of every man since. Adam felt naked before Eve after his disobedience, but more so before the eyes of God, hiding from Him in terror. His nakedness is ours. His terror is ours as well. Shame is a sharp reminder of our loss of glory, like a splinter we cannot ignore or remove. Any sense of strength and wisdom we attain is only a covering for what we truly feel—weak and foolish. We are not men, and we know it.

Seen in this light, our search to become heroic is a desperate attempt to recover that lost glory by any means possible. Go back to the nightmare of showing up in public with only your underwear on. What would be your first response? To coolly assess the situation and make the most prudent choice? Hardly. You frantically hide until you find some clothes. This is the urgency we feel. We have to find a covering, and we have to find it now—whatever the means, whatever the cost. So we latch onto anything that appears to offer us some level of greatness. But what we latch onto deceives us. It's not what we thought.

It's false glory.

A PICTURE OF FALSE GLORY

I clearly remember the first time I saw *Chariots of Fire*, the Oscar-winning biopic of Eric Liddell, the flying Scotsman who won the 400m in the 1924 Olympics. Watching him on the screen, I felt the fire burn inside of me. Here was a true hero who seemed to have found glory. I saw it in his unflagging determination to train, his refusal to race the 100m prelims on Sunday, and his shocking win of the 400m in world-record time. As a former track coach, I know that his race forever changed the 400m. It was usually a paced run with a sprint at the end, but Eric went out full throttle from the beginning, torching his competitors at the 200m mark and hanging on to win. From that time on, the 400m was run as a sprint. The sheer pluck to risk something like that and pull it off felt so heroic to me. But his true glory was not found in Olympic gold. He left for China the next year as a missionary, where he eventually became interned in a POW camp as Japan occupied China. Here, he was a constant source of encouragement to others, setting up a school and sporting activities for the children imprisoned there. Those in the camp experienced Eric as a man full of good humor and winsome charm. Sadly, his own life ended from a brain tumor before the Allied troops could rescue him. His last recorded words were these: "It's complete surrender." It was a reference to how he had offered his whole life to God. Eric never seemed to latch on to his incredible speed to feel strong. He didn't have to win glory. He already had it from God. As I watched the movie, I wanted to be just like Eric. But back in real life, I was Harold.

Harold Abrahams was the foil in the movie, the English sprinter who was determined to show that those with a Semitic background could make it into the upper echelons of power. He was out to prove himself, no matter how he must train, even if he had to break with Olympic tradition and hire a professional coach. He also constantly compared himself to Eric, sometimes jealous, sometimes afraid of him. When the Olympics began, he found out about Eric's refusal to race on Sunday and realized he wouldn't have to compete against him after all. He ran the 100m and won. But it was a hollow victory. He got the gold medal, but left the track alone, unsung by anyone except his fiancé. It had all been about him. He won Olympic glory all right, but it was false glory.

Like Harold, I, too, ran after false glory, deceived by it again and again. The stories of chasing fame I have already mentioned are a clear testament to this drive, but one story is left to tell. When I set my sights on becoming an author a number of years ago, I felt like Harold. I was jealous of authors and consumed with getting my own book published. I was out to prove that I had what it took to be a great writer. When I finally landed a book deal from a publisher, I felt I had achieved success. I had won glory. I had daydreams about book reviews that would call my work a classic. Yet instead of feeling settled in the success, my drive to compete only intensified. Now I had to get the word out and convince others to buy my book. Next I had to work harder to get a second book published. This meant more prestigious endorsements, more buzz, more reviews. It was the same pattern all over again. Instead of affirmation, I felt pressure. Being an author never gave me what I thought it would.

Most of us are only ready to hear another option when we see the damage we have inflicted on others or reach a breaking point ourselves. I distinctly remember the moment I realized that my success as a track coach wasn't working. Instead of feeling affirmed as a man, I felt exhausted. If I didn't stop coaching, I knew I would destroy myself or my marriage—or both. I had reached the breaking point and was ready to listen to another option.

That option is presented throughout the pages of the Bible, but it is summed up succinctly by the prophet Jeremiah: "'Let not the wise boast of their wisdom or the strong boast of their strength or the rich boast of their riches, but let the one who boasts boast about this: that they have the understanding to know me, that I am the LORD, who exercises kindness, justice and righteousness on earth, for in these I delight,' declares the LORD" (Jer. 9:23–24). The words resonate. They speak truth. Whatever we boast in—strength or wisdom or riches—is a covering. It's what we lean on for some sense of heroic glory. But it's a sham. There is another option if we are ready to hear it. It is to boast in God, to experience Him as the One who loves kindness and justice. This is the wellspring of true glory. This is the fountainhead of true manhood.

But this only raises more questions: How do we get there? How do we escape the trap of false glory? How do we learn to boast in God and find true glory there? And how will all this make us heroic? To answer these questions, we must now take a side path.

CHAPTER 4

A GLIMMER IN THE DARKNESS

*"And Man as a whole, Man pitted against
the universe, have we seen him at all till we
see that he is like a hero in a fairy tale?"*
—C. S. Lewis quote from "A Review of J. R. R.
Tolkien's *The Lord of the Rings*"

*"We sit in the mud, my friend,
and reach for the stars."*
—Ivan Turgenev, *Fathers and Sons*

*He trains my hands for battle;
my arms can bend a bow of bronze.
You make your saving help my shield,
and your right hand sustains me;
your help has made me great.*
—Psalm 18:34–35

The seismic quakes in a man's soul often come at the most unexpected moments.

One of those moments happened while attending a reception at a friend's home over the Christmas holidays. As the crowd waned, I wandered off into an adjacent room to look through the books displayed for guests. My eyes brushed over some positioned on a glass coffee table, but nothing caught my attention. I then moved to a small side table posted by the front door. On it were several books neatly tucked between decorative bookends. One with an antique cloth cover intrigued me. I pulled it out and opened the cover. I was soon so immersed in its contents that I forgot where I was or how long I had been reading. The sound of Heidi's voice in the next room finally pulled me up out of my reverie. I had by then only made it through the introduction, so I asked my friend if I could take it home to finish. The rest of the book ended up being a children's version of Greek mythology. But those tales agitated something. I felt the ground quake inside of me.

The story of Jason and the Argonauts journeying for the Golden Fleece touched the longing to be trained for a great work and to do it with other men. The story of Theseus doing something courageous to win his father's love pierced me with hope about my own father. The tale of Perseus slaying the Gorgon spoke to the desire to do something worthy in life, even if it meant facing death. I was so mesmerized by these stories that I ordered my own copy to read them again.

I had probably read these same tales during Greek mythology class in the eighth grade. But now many years later, they took on the aura of something transcendent and true, something that gleamed through all the errors of Greek polytheism. That something is encapsulated in the title I first saw embossed on the spine of that antique cloth book—*The Greek Heroes*.

There it is. *Heroes.*

It was the heroic in these stories that shook me awake.

The awakening happens because we are, by and large, asleep as men. It's as if we have put ourselves under a sleeping spell to survive—and with good reason. The heart of a boy, and later that of a young man, is captivated by the heroic men in his life, only to be disappointed or heartbroken by them at some point. They cannot stay on the lofty pedestal on which he has placed them. Our own attempts to become heroes as men get us no further. We get hopelessly entangled in the mess we create. With such a failure record, it seems perfectly sensible to forget such an unmanageable longing. It only wreaks pain and confusion. Wouldn't it be better to just settle down and get on with the rest of life? There's plenty to do with marriage and children, careers and finances, yard work and house repair, plenty to fill a man's heart and time. Why bother with something that gets us into trouble? So we put ourselves to sleep—or so we think.

But the heroic longing erupts, unbidden, in the least likely of places—in story. We find ourselves no longer asleep but jarred awake and in tears, burning again to be that hero. This is exactly what happened to me with those Greek myths. Those stories were calling out to me: *Wake up! You have forgotten who you are. You have forgotten what you are to do. Your life is meant to be so much more than what you think.*

I felt the fire in the call. The heat radiated off the page. I wanted to burn.

THE RESONANCE OF STORY

What happened to me with those Greek myths began many years earlier in the fifth and sixth grades. I loved the teacher I had for both of those years—Mrs. Duncan. The last period was always spent reading a story to us. No matter how tired or distracted we were after a day of school, she would calmly ask us to sit in our desks in that overcrowded portable. Then as we heard the sound of her voice start the story, the magic would happen. We would listen in rapt attention, transported away to uncharted worlds of adventure. I still remember the titles of two of those books: *From the Mixed-Up Files of Mrs. Basil E. Frankweiler* and *A Wrinkle in Time*, classics still read today. The enchantment must have stayed with me after school hours because somewhere during that time I attempted to read *The Lord of the Rings* on my own. The smell of the freshly printed pages would mix with the quiet of my bedroom as I sat and entered the strange world of hobbits. But I got bogged down halfway through and gave up. Yet my early plunge into story etched something into me.

During adolescence, the etching wore thin in English classes with assignments to read books that felt irrelevant. It was then buried by my later training in philosophy and theology. I believed then that concepts and ideas held the magic. Stories were for children, not for thinking, mature men. I never stated it like that, but I felt it nonetheless. However, in my mid-thirties during an especially turbulent period, I rediscovered story. Somewhere in that time, I picked up *The Lord of the*

Rings, more than twenty years after my first attempt. Heidi had finished reading it, and perhaps that was the impetus to get me started. This time as I entered the story, I awakened to the enchantment once again. Feelings long ago buried resurfaced at unscripted moments—and those feelings clustered around Frodo.

Frodo is the most unlikely character to be chosen as the ringbearer. He's a hobbit, a small creature of Middle Earth, who loves his daily victuals and pipe weed. Like all hobbits, he wants to live a quiet life and stay out of trouble. Trouble comes to him anyway. He inherits the mysterious ring of his uncle Bilbo, only to find that it is the one master ring that can put all Middle Earth in Sauron's grip. His job is now the impossible task of destroying the ring by taking it back to where it was forged—inside the volcanic fire and heat of Mount Doom.

The story is so familiar now to millions. What wasn't familiar was the resonance it struck inside me. My whole life has been plagued with a shadowy sense that I am to bear something, that I have some mission to accomplish even if it looks impossible. As I read Frodo's story, it became my story. I began to look for clues as to how to live by watching Frodo. I saw him find traveling companions, trust his mentor Gandalf, fight opposition from all sides, push through confusion, refuse to capitulate, face gnawing fear, and finally surrender his life to complete the mission—all of these clues and more I inwardly digested. Frodo's life became a blueprint for mine.

He became my hero.

It's important to remember that I did this without any prompting or instruction. I didn't need that. I just knew the story was saying something true, that Frodo was living something true. When we think in the world of concepts, these must be demonstrated as true through argument, following steps that the mind can grasp and approve. But stories just ring true, and the movie form of stories only heightens the resonance. Now we can watch the story come to life with actors that move and breathe.

I love to ask men about their favorite movies and characters. The expected ones always come out. Who isn't taken by the courage of William Wallace in *Braveheart*? Who isn't lit up by the determination of Maximus in *Gladiator*? Who isn't stung by the sacrifice of Captain Miller in *Saving Private Ryan*? The movie list continues with *Shawshank Redemption*, *Field of Dreams*, *The King's Speech*, *Cinderella Man*, *Lone Survivor*, *The Patriot*, *Schindler's List*, and many others. But something always happens as we generate the movie list. There is an energy generated in our conversation. It's the energy of praise for the heroes we admire.

That energy is especially apparent in the stories we return to again and again. We felt the resonance there once and keep returning to it, hoping for more. One friend confessed to me that he had watched the very first *Star Wars* movie fourteen times when it first came out. He even got a job at a movie theater so that he could keep watching it after his initial viewing on the big screen. His heart was riveted to Luke Skywalker, a young man who had lost his family and his way. As my friend watched Obi-Wan come for Luke and train him, he longed to have a man come for him as well, coach him, and take him on adventures. He wanted Luke's story to become his.

I have repeatedly returned to *The Lord of the Rings* over the past twenty years, both in book and movie form. While preparing to teach this material, I went back to the movie to pull out some clips for viewing. One of them showed Frodo's struggle with the Ringwraiths and his desire to give up. The task was too hard. The burden was too heavy. Yet with Sam's encouragement, he got back up on his feet, determined to plod on. As I watched, I felt the resonance once again. Frodo's struggle became mine. Four years earlier, I had started a ministry to men with high hopes. I was being asked to bear something and accomplish a mission. The initial call was intoxicating. But the ensuing years were pockmarked with so many failures that I was tempted to quit. The task was too hard. The opposition too formidable. All of this surfaced as I watched Frodo. I felt the deep reverberations. Then Frodo's determination suddenly became mine, and I was ready to plod on.

He had once again become my hero.

THE STORY BEHIND THE STORY

But what exactly is going on with us in story? Why the resonance? What happens to us in those moments of awakening? Let's start by looking at the narrative structure of story. The answer to our questions comes in the name given to that structure, "The Heroic Journey." What makes a story even possible is a hero. Perhaps you remember something about this from English class in high school or college. The hero is the main character who is called out to go and achieve something. This is his quest, his heroic journey. The story then threads itself through external enemies the hero fights and internal flaws he faces. There are twists and turns in the plot, defeats and victories, as he keeps pressing toward his goal. After a final confrontation with his chief adversary, the hero finally accomplishes his quest, living out his true identity.

Let's take a couple of well-known stories and see how this works. In *Gladiator*, Maximus is the great hero, the general who has the love and respect of the entire Roman army. He is asked by the emperor Marcus Aurelius to become his successor and save Rome from its political corruption. This is to be his new quest. But Aurelius's son, the scheming Commodus, murders his father and orders Maximus executed. Maximus escapes, only to find that his wife and son have been crucified by Commodus. He now becomes a gladiator, seeking revenge for what Commodus as done. The story tumbles through conflicts and battles to a final fight scene between the two of them. Here Maximus kills Commodus and orders that justice be restored to Rome as Aurelius had wished. But it happens at the price of his life. He dies honored as a hero.

Here's another example from one of the most popular musicals, seen by more than seventy million people, *Les Misérables*. The hero, Jean Valjean, is an ex-convict who receives unexpected grace at the hands of a priest. Instead of being taken back to prison for stealing his silverware, Valjean is spared by the priest, who lies to the police and hands Valjean his silver candlesticks as well. Along with this extravagant gift, the priest summons him to live a new life for God and the good of others. This becomes Valjean's heroic journey. He does this by becoming a wealthy mayor and using his means to uplift the poor. But the story takes a twist when he seeks to help the prostitute Fantine and her daughter Cosette, both in desperate circumstances. His attempt to assist them exposes him to his adversary Javert, who recognizes Valjean as a former convict he knew while working in the same prison. The rest of the story is now an endless series of near defeats and conflicts for Valjean. The final vindication comes as Javert commits suicide, unable to handle how Valjean spared his own life during a political rebellion. At the end, Valjean dies, having saved Cosette's lover, giving them both hope for a better life. This hero truly gave all he had for the good of others.

These two examples reveal the mechanics of how the heroic journey works out in stories. But it doesn't convey the power they carry. I first saw *Gladiator* in the theater with a high school friend. On the ride home, he told me that he burned to be like Maximus. He longed to be the warrior that fights for something eternal. Every time I see *Les Misérables*, I weep at the end, even though I know the story. I am so drawn to Valjean's noble heart, choosing at every turn the good of others over his.

I have only given a brief sketch of the heroic journey, one that has been analyzed by scholars and parsed out into varying steps. One of the most widely known of these analyses comes from the research of Joseph

Campbell. He gave the heroic journey a new name, the Monomyth. For Campbell, the story of the hero is the one story endlessly retold in both ancient myth and modern fiction. To explore this idea more, I scheduled an interview with an English teacher colleague. I sat in a classroom desk like one of her students, scribbling on a notepad I had brought. Much of our conversation was stimulating, but one thing she said I will never forget. My question was simple: "How prevalent is the heroic journey in literature?" Her response came as soon as my last word left my mouth: "The heroic journey *is* literature."

There is only one story, the story of the hero.

But the one story can take many forms: a journey into self-discovery and awareness, a journey to live for something higher than oneself, a journey to discover one's family or heritage, a journey to discover loss and deal with it, a journey to overcome evil and injustice. This variety yields endless possibilities for creating stories and the heroes in them. Yet all of these journeys closely follow two thematic guideposts: identity and quest. Somewhere along the way, the hero accepts who he is and what he is to do. What makes the story grip us is his determination to live out that identity and quest, whatever the obstacles, whatever the sacrifices. This is exactly why Frodo's story gripped me. He realized that he was more than an orphaned hobbit, taken in by his uncle Bilbo, to live out his days peacefully in the Shire. He was the ringbearer and had to find a way to destroy the ring, even if it meant letting his life go in the process. This expanding sense of identity and purpose form the underpinnings of any tale. It's what makes the hero heroic.

But the journey of the hero is not just a literary structure to be dissected in English class. Stories reflect something true about reality. That's why we feel the resonance. When we see a heroic man in action, we don't just want to watch the story. We want to enter it. In that moment, we are being summoned.

We are being called to take our own heroic journey.

Such a proposition can at first resurrect long-buried hopes: *Really? Is it possible? Is it true? Am I being called to become like the heroes I have loved?* But soon, the cynical side asserts itself: *Such thinking is impractical. Frankly it's ridiculous. Stories are child's play, a momentary escape from the stress of daily life. Why spoil the fun of stories with a bunch of dreamy-eyed hopes?* But our objections cover something else besides lost hope. They cover fear. To open ourselves to the heroic journey is to face the incalculable. It is the end of our best-laid schemes for security in this life: *Good Lord, I could be asked to do anything. So many of the great heroes ended up dying. What will it cost me? What opposition will I have to face? Where will this all lead?* And now the real issue is exposed.

What every man longs to be is also his greatest fear.

PROBING DEEPER

Let's sort out our conflicted feelings by probing deeper into the heroic journey. Why is there only one story, the story of the hero? What does this say about the nature of reality? And what does the heroic journey have to do with God, the ultimate reality? The one story behind all literature reflects reality because we are all created in the image of the Great Storyteller, God Himself. The knowledge of His reality and glory is imprinted on every man, yet we have all turned away from Him. In so doing, we simply replaced the one true God with thousands of man-made gods: "They exchanged the truth about God for a lie, and worshiped and served created things rather than the Creator—who is forever praised" (Rom. 1:25). Every man is a compulsive idolater, bowing down with groveling submission to success, power, fame—anything that will replace that lost glory.

The imprint of His glory, though now faint and disfigured, still remains—felt in our deepest desires. It is those deep longings that get stirred in story. Those stories also contain faint glimmers of that same glory, like sunbeams suddenly breaking through a darkening cloud bank. In our best stories, the beams shine with astonishing power. Listen to Tolkien, the creator of *The Lord of the Rings*, on this very point:

> We have come from God, and inevitably the myths woven by us, though they contain error, will also reflect a splintered fragment of the true light, the eternal truth that is with God. Indeed only by myth-making, only by becoming "sub-creator" and inventing stories, can Man aspire to the state of perfection that he knew before the Fall.[2]

Remember the surest thing a man knows about himself is that he is not a man. What the great stories do is give us a fleeting glimpse of a real man, one who seems untainted by the fall. The imprint still left in us awakens at the sight of such a man. We tremble with hope and desire. In that moment, we are being called back home to our rightful selves. We also give that man a name.

We call him a hero.

More insight on this point comes from the great Story itself, the Bible. When we open its pages, we find men being called out by God to do something for His kingdom. One of my favorite stories is the Gideon narrative from the book of Judges. It begins with the impossible situation in which the Israelites find themselves because of their continued rebellion. God hands them over to the Midianites, who overrun their homeland. Then as the Israelites come to their senses and cry out to the Lord for help, He acts— but not like anyone could have predicted. What He does in this most desperate of situations is to call out the most unlikely of men, the baby of a family, whose clan was the weakest of his tribe. An angel approaches Gideon with a greeting that must have rocked him: "The LORD is with you, mighty warrior" (6:12). I'm sure Gideon thought the angel must have mistaken him for someone else. His objections come swiftly: "Pardon me, my lord," Gideon replied, "but if the LORD is with us, why has all this happened to us? Where are all his wonders that our ancestors told us about when they said, 'Did not the LORD bring us up out of Egypt?' But now the LORD has abandoned us and given us into the hand of Midian" (6:13). The angel sidesteps these grievances and drives straight to the point: "Go in the strength you have and save Israel out of Midian's hand. Am I not sending you?" (6:14). Gideon continues to object and has to be given signs along the way that God is really sending him—first by fire that consumes meat and bread, then by a woolen fleece that is dew-soaked one morning on dry ground, only to be dry the next morning on dew-soaked ground. The tangible proofs solidify Gideon's wavering faith. He moves out and obeys the Lord's call. The rest of the tale in Judges 6–7 sounds like something out of one of your favorite war movies: impossible odds, heart-stopping tension, daring feats. But in the end, the Midianites are conquered.

We are also told throughout the story that it is the Lord who keeps setting the stage for Gideon so that he could accomplish his mission. God is the One who really saved the day, the true Hero of the tale, as He is of every Old Testament story. But—and this is an extremely important *but*—He invites Gideon to play a huge role in the tale—fearful, wavering Gideon. He does this by giving Gideon from the very start those two critical elements of all heroic journeys: identity and quest. His identity: mighty warrior. His quest: defeat the Midianites. What God seems to be doing is startling. He invites Gideon to become a hero under His coaching. God sets the stage, but Gideon must play his part. In that invitation is something even more startling. God apparently wants Gideon to share in His glory. He wants Gideon to become more of the man he truly is, not the cowering farmer we find as the story opens.

He does that by calling Gideon out to take a heroic journey.

Gideon's heroic quest is repeated in all the great characters of the Old Testament: Abraham, Moses, David, Elijah, Jeremiah, Nehemiah, and many others. It's a chorus that keeps being repeated. God is the great Hero, but He also calls men out to be heroic under His tutelage. He calls them out to taste their glory as men. That's how He gets glory.

THE RETURN TO THE OLD SELF

But with that said, is it enough? Remember where we are. Our heroes have failed us. Our attempts to be heroes have failed us. With such a dismal track record, can the inspiration we feel with heroic stories save us, even stories from God's Word? Can the heart-grip we feel and the tears that come translate back into the grind of work deadlines, marital spats, and monthly bills?

You already know the answer. Those moments fade almost as quickly as they come. After the credits roll or the book closes, we return back to something much more familiar—the old self. Remember the inspiration I felt with Eric Liddell? When the movie ended, I wanted to rise up and conquer the world. I wanted to live heroically, daring great feats for God. My heart screamed out, *Yes, yes, yes! This is the man I want to become.* But as the feeling faded, the rush of daily life swept back over me. I soon returned to my old self, to the role of Harold Abrahams, to the man fixated on proving himself by his success. You know how a boomerang works.

No matter how hard or high you throw, it will return back to the same place. This is what happens in those moments of inspiration. Our longings hurtle us into the air, only to find ourselves plummeting back to earth. There is no forward motion, just deflated hope.

But what if the point of these stories was only to hurtle us high? What if they were never meant to be more? What if their purpose was to be a neon-blinking signpost, planted in our deep desires by God Himself, pointing out the type of men we were meant to be? What if these stories were never intended to be the power to change us but the slap to awaken us? If that's the case, they have done their job well. To ask more would be to expect what they cannot give.

To find the power to change, we must look elsewhere, to another unlikely man who became a hero.

CHAPTER 5

THE GREAT HERO

*"All the armies that ever marched, and all
the navies that were ever built, and all the
parliaments that ever sat, and all the kings
that ever reigned, put together, have not
affected the life of man upon the earth as
powerfully as has this one solitary life."*
—James Allan Francis quoted from a sermon titled
"Arise, Sir Knight"

*"The heart of Christianity is a myth which is also
a fact. The old myth of the Dying God, without
ceasing to be a myth, comes down from the heaven
of legend and imagination to the earth of history."*
—C. S. Lewis quoted in *God in the Dock*

*And he is the head of the body, the church; he is the
beginning and the firstborn from among the dead,
so that in everything, he might have the supremacy.*
—Colossians 1:18

To be ashamed of someone you love feels like an act of treachery. I should know. It's been my story.

My freshman high school English class met in a nondescript classroom crowded with dreary wooden desks imprisoned by whitewashed walls. The class must have been just as dreary because, to this day, I remember nothing about it. But one incident stands out in Technicolor relief.

My faith in Jesus had recently become real to me, and I had gotten involved in a ministry geared toward sharing that faith with others. We were given booklets to hand out that spoke about Jesus. I must have tucked a handful of them in one of my books to take to school, but I don't remember having any plan to hand them out. What I do remember is what happened one morning before that English class began. As I sat down in my usual seat and put my books on top of the desk, one of them must have been precariously placed because it fell onto the floor, the one with all the booklets inside. They went flying everywhere. I was horrified. If my peers saw them, I feared being labeled a religious nut. I could feel a wave of crimson sweep over my face. Frantically, I picked the booklets up and stuffed them wherever they would be hidden. One friend sitting next to me tried to be helpful and began picking them up. In my embarrassment, I snatched them quickly out of his hands. That morning I escaped being associated with Jesus. But the shame I felt continued to prick me. Why was I ashamed of Him? What was it about Jesus that made me feel unacceptable to others?

You have to understand my inner life as a young man. I was shy beyond words and lived in constant dread of being ridiculed by my peers. I saw what happened to students who were at the bottom of the pecking order. I never wanted to find myself there. So I tried as best as I could to stay ordinary. To step out of social expectations meant harassment and exclusion. Jesus didn't fit those expectations.

The one time I did get the courage to associate with Jesus happened in another class, this time history. The teacher loved to poke at others with sarcastic jabs. I never wanted to be one of his targets. Despite my fear of him, I decided to make a comment about Jesus in one of the papers I wrote. I thought it was relevant to the topic, and it was a chance to show my colors discreetly. He did not see it that way. When he handed out the graded papers, he held up mine and pronounced in front of the class with some disgust: "Delvaux, you need to get off of your high preachin' horse." The jab sunk deep. Shamed by an authority figure, I went into hiding again. But the hiding always felt like treachery.

The shame manifested itself during college in a slightly different way. Public discourse was accepted in and out of the classroom on a wide variety of topics, even ones that had once appeared taboo. But to bring up Jesus was the ultimate blunder. One's personal religious beliefs were just that—personal and, thus, illegitimate for class discussion. I had now run into the strong cross-pressure of living in a secular age. It felt like a gale force wind relentlessly pushing me where I did not want to go. The university system, birthed inside of the church in England nearly one thousand years ago, now had little place for religious dialogue, and no place for conversation about Jesus. He had been banished. Indeed, the irony is much larger. So much of what we call Western civilization finds its roots and footing in the person of

Jesus. Yet He was no longer an acceptable part of civilized discussion.

But understanding the irony never solved the quandary. I continued to feel shame about Jesus even through seminary and into the ministry. I could preach about Him with gusto in church, but felt timid about Him the rest of the week. To mention His name felt like trying to push open a metal door rusted shut for years. Something was blocking me. It was easier to stay quiet. I excused myself by saying that I was no evangelist. But the sense of shame hung over me like an ominous cloud. No matter what pep talks I gave myself, I could not shake the deepening sense of treachery I felt. How could I be ashamed of the One who had done so much for me?

I know now that I am not alone in my dilemma. Many men in the church are conflicted about Him as well. We do not feel about Him the way we feel about our heroes. And we don't know why.

THE HERO WE LOVE

The dilemma becomes more pointed when we turn to another man, one universally loved by all men. Before *Braveheart* was filmed, William Wallace was an obscure Scot renegade from the dim shadows of the Middle Ages. But since the movie's release in 1995, he has become a household word synonymous with bravery. The film continues to electrify men. The reason is simple: Wallace is the epitome of the noble hero.

Here is a man who stands up to evil and fights for the freedom of his people while other Scots cower in fear.

He is willing to give his life, if necessary, so that freedom can be won. He is not interested in titles or power. All he wants is release from the grip of British tyranny for his people. Listen to him as he addresses the warring nobles of Scotland: "There is a difference between us. You think the people of this country exist to provide you with position. I think your position exists to provide the people with freedom. And I go to make sure that they have it." And then his conversation with Robert the Bruce, the heir to the Scottish throne: "Nobles? What does that mean—to be noble? Your title gives you claim to the throne of our country. But men don't follow titles, they follow courage!" It is that courage that sets the hearts of his Scottish brethren on fire. After his torture and death, they go out and beat the British at the battle of Bannockburn, winning their freedom, despite being outmatched and outnumbered. They had felt the glory of a true hero and been forever marked by it.

The story is so well known that it doesn't bear further mention. What is not so well known is the story behind the story. The screenplay writer of *Braveheart*, Randall Wallace (no direct lineage to William Wallace), had other career aspirations as a young man. He had entertained the ministry and even attended seminary, yet with the encouragement of his pastor, who sensed his gifts and calling, Randall moved to California to pursue his passion of writing screenplays and directing films. When asked why he liked to write about heroes, here's what he said: "Doesn't everybody love stories about heroes? They grab our attention, they make our hearts pound—but only if we believe them, only if we can identify with them in some way and hope that to some extent we can become more like them."[3] Yes, that's the resonance we feel with heroic stories.

But how did he convince Mel Gibson to make a movie about an unknown Scottish knight? Here's how he pitched it to Mel: "Every story has a message, and what most movies tell us is that the guy with the bluest eyes and the cutest dimples and the biggest biceps is the one who wins. What this story says is if you are faithful to your heart, even if they cut it out of you, you prevail. That's the story I want my sons to see."[4] Mel was so compelled by the story that he not only directed the movie but also played the lead role as Wallace himself.

The movie is revered by men everywhere, especially those who share Randall's faith. Here is his thinking on this point: "I believe Christians have embraced that film because the heart of the story is in fact a Christian heart."[5] Indeed, William Wallace echoes the heart of that one Man who went through torture and death on a cross for the freedom of His people. We love Wallace precisely *because* he was a little like Jesus. Listen to Randall once again: "Jesus is the ultimate hero. His message in the face of unspeakable suffering—spiritual, physical and mental—was, 'You can try to kill my body, but I will never deny who I am.'"[6] For Randall, Jesus was the great Hero.

A STRANGE DISCONNECT

Yet for so many men, even those in the church, He doesn't feel like the great Hero. They can gush over

Wallace, but with Jesus they feel unsure. They may believe He is the Son of God and the Lord of their lives. They may worship Him at church and pray to Him at home. But to admire Jesus as the great Hero? To love Him as the ultimate noble Man? The idea feels strange, even alien. But if He is the great Hero, why the disconnect? Why the shame? What's going on here? Here are some of the culprits.

First, the warrior image for men feels like the strong man at his best. William Wallace came as a warrior with a massive broadsword, using it to mow down the enemy. But Jesus did not brandish a sword. He didn't charge the hill. He didn't come and clean house with the Romans who ruled Israel at the time, despite the fact that many believed He would. There is one place where a sword was used around Jesus. When a mob came to arrest Him, Peter tried to protect His beloved leader with a sword he had brought. He swung it, lopping off the ear of one of the high priest's servants. Jesus' response was sharp: "Put your sword away!" (John 18:10–11). Jesus doesn't appear to be a warrior. He didn't even put up a fight.

This apparent lack of fighting spirit is compounded by our poor images of Him. Some of this may be due to misguided paintings and illustrations that picture Him as kind but insipid, even sickly and emaciated. Rather than being at the vortex of controversy, striking love and fear into the hearts of men, as the New Testament presents Him, He comes across visually as enigmatic and wispy, even a little weird. Some of this may reflect a poor theology of Jesus, portraying His divinity in a way that it undermines His humanity. Such thinking is a part of the Gnostic heresy that infiltrated the church from the earliest days. Its tentacles still reach and poison minds today, two millennia later. Bottom line: He may be Jesus, but He's not a man we want to be like.

Underneath our poor images of Jesus is another culprit, one harder to pull up, yet more potent because of its covertness. The apostle Paul put it this way: "The god of this age has blinded the minds of unbelievers, so that they cannot see the light of the gospel that displays the glory of Christ, who is the image of God" (2 Cor. 4:4). Paul spoke here about the blinding that happens to those who will not believe. A veil has been pulled over their eyes so that they cannot see the glory of Jesus, much less share it with Him. The devil is behind this, clouding thought and smearing truth. I believe one of his schemes is to impress images of Jesus on the minds of men that are decidedly unmasculine. Even for men who have seen the glory of Christ and believe, they can still be oppressed by this scheme. The result? A man may say he believes in Jesus, but in his heart he will look for his heroes elsewhere.

SKETCHING A BETTER IMAGE

Even when these culprits are brought to the light, we need more. We need a better image of Jesus, one that illuminates His heroic nobleness. Let's try to sketch this out first by noting something in the structure of the Bible itself. In every Old Testament narrative, by direct statement or implicit understanding, God is the great Hero. It's not the human characters that loom so large in the narratives—Abraham, Moses, David, Elijah, and others. As influential as these men were, they were deeply flawed, and the Old Testament is shockingly honest about their flaws. Only God is the mighty Warrior. Only He is the Hero who comes in the nick of time to save the day. In a tight parallel, Jesus appears in the New Testament. He is the centerpiece of the Gospels and the driving force behind the letters. All conversations point to Him. All debates center around Him. All eyes turn toward Him. This is in crisp contrast to the closest men around Him, His disciples. They appear weak and wavering throughout the Gospels. Only after the touch of His Holy Spirit do they find the power that pushes them out to set the world on fire. It is Jesus who is the focal point of the New Testament, the Hero in every story, doing exactly what God did in the Old Testament. The implication is difficult to avoid. God has shown up in history as a man to turn the tide of evil and save the day.

There is another point that adds depth to this image. Remember the heroic journey that forms the backbone of all literature. Here the hero, the main character, goes on a journey to do something worthy and just. He holds to that quest despite the obstacles, even if it costs him deeply. In accomplishing the mission, the hero lives out his true identity, now known to himself and others. Identity and quest are the underpinnings that frame the heroic journey.

It only takes a glance at the New Testament to see that Jesus lived this journey. Identity—yes. He knew precisely who He was. If one thing is patently clear from the Gospels, it is this: Jesus was His own man. He did not cater to the whims of popularity. He did not curry approval to grab power. He burst the constricting molds in which everyone tried to place him. No one could figure out who He was. But Jesus knew. He was the beloved Son of the Father. Quest—absolutely yes. He didn't come to fix political corruption or wipe out poverty, as laudable as those goals are. He came to save the world from sin in the only way possible—taking that sin upon Himself. It was this passion that drove Him day and night through His earthly ministry to the torture of the cross.

No story better illustrates that razor-sharp sense of identity and quest than the temptation narrative (Matt. 4:1–11). Here Jesus is alone in the desert and weakened by nearly six weeks without food. The deceiver now shows up with this: "If you are the Son of God, tell these stones to become bread" (v. 3). The devil has gone for the jugular, seeking to derail His identity and mission. If Jesus is really the unique Son of God, if that is His identity, then surely He could use a little of God's immense power to satisfy His hunger with a miracle. It's such a small thing. No one would know. But for Jesus, it strikes at the root of His purpose. His mission is to use the power given Him to serve others, never for His own benefit. The next two temptations work the same point from different angles. The devil is circling his opponent to discover any weak place. But there is none. Jesus stands. The devil leaves. Jesus knew who He was and was determined to complete His mission. Nothing would stop Him. Not misunderstanding, criticism, torture, or death. In a stunning way, we see Jesus embodying the heroic journey. The hero climbed out of mythology, taken on muscle and breath, and become a man. His personality is so commanding that a hero is sometimes called a Christ figure.

Let's turn to Tolkien again at this point. He believed that when we read the great heroic stories and myths, our hearts are spellbound with a proper enchantment, one that awakens us to the good and the true. I have already told my story of awakening with the Greek myths. This is the purpose of such stories, including ones we call fairy tales. But when he turns his attention to the story of Jesus, he says this: "The Gospels contain a fairy-story, or a story of a larger kind which embraces all the essence of fairy-stories. They contain many marvels—peculiarly artistic, beautiful, and moving; 'mythical' in their perfectly self-contained significance."[6] In other words, all that we have loved in the great stories is also in the story of Jesus. But this story is the one fairy tale that actually happened.

When we step back to look at our newly sketched image of Jesus, we can now see it. He is the great hero. He consistently uses His power and wisdom for the good of others. All throughout the Gospels, He is fighting for others, lifting the yoke of injustice, setting the captive free, healing the sick and blind, loving the poor and outcast, teaching all who would listen, and confronting His enemies fearlessly. He speaks the truth and refuses to recant, even when it leads to His death.

There is more. Jesus is the *man*—the ideal man—masculinity awakening and surging forth in its potent form. The Scriptures say that He is the head of a new humanity. Where Adam fell, He stood. Where Adam was defeated, He conquered. Great men have always left their mark, etching themselves into the hearts of others. Jesus was that greatest of men. Whatever He did, wherever He went, He marked others with the slap of His masculine vigor, His abounding energy, and His indomitable passion. If you spent any time with Him, you were marked forever. It was the mark of glory. John put it this way: "The Word became flesh and made his dwelling among us. We have seen his glory, the glory of the one and only Son, who came from the Father, full of grace and truth" (John 1:14). The Son of God enfleshed Himself to show men what a true man was.

No story shows that noble greatness better than a small vignette from His suffering on the cross. He is in the last throes of dying. He has braved the brutal flogging that left His back in bloody shreds. He has endured the huge spikes impaling His wrists—missing arteries so that He dies slowly, but hitting nerves, sending jolts of pain up and down His arms. Every breath required Him to do the unthinkable—to push Himself up on those nails, again and again. Men who were crucified were known to scream and curse in agony. But Jesus wasn't doing any of that. He was thinking of others.

Everyone had fled the horrific scene, deserting Jesus, except for some women, His mother, and John. We can only imagine the torment Mary must have felt. But in the midst of the torture, He wanted to offer whatever comfort He could. So looking at Mary and John, He said first to Mary, "Woman, here is your son." Then to John, "Here is your mother." The One abandoned by friends and followers wanted to make sure that His mother wasn't abandoned (John 19:25–27). When I think about such heroic love, I am moved beyond words.

THE WARRIOR INCOGNITO

One point is still left to be resolved. What about the warrior? How could Jesus be the great hero if He refused to put up the fight? But this is where His greatness shines even brighter. What we see in Jesus is glory, but it's veiled glory. It's strength, but submitted strength. There was one place where that glory and strength were unveiled for a fleeting moment: in the silence of a mountaintop with His three closest disciples. In that transfiguration, they saw the searing light, His dazzling countenance, and the conversation with Moses and Elijah. But just as soon as the veil was lifted, it was placed back. The glory faded, and they descended the mountaintop (Mark 9:2–8).

That veil then stayed in place all the way through the cross. The taunts hurled by the religious leaders as He hung there were so much like those the deceiver used in the desert: "You who are going to destroy the temple and build it in three days, save yourself! Come down from the cross, if you are the Son of God!" (Matt. 27:40). There it is again. *If this is your real identity, use your power for your own good. Show us a miracle like that, and then we'll believe.* The cruelty of such barbs can hardly be imagined. But Jesus would not give in. He would not use His strength for that purpose. He refused to fight to save His life. He would let it go to save others.

Jesus chose to lay aside His glory for our good. Instead of a warrior, He came as a servant, one with the hidden strength of a warrior pulsating under the surface. Paul explains it this way: "Who, being in very nature God, did not consider equality with God something to be used to his own advantage; rather, he made himself nothing by taking the very nature of a servant, being made in human likeness" (Phil. 2:6–7). The warrior came incognito. It was the only way He could complete the quest.

But there will come a day when the servant will become the warrior. The veil will be lifted. All will see and be in awe:

> I saw heaven standing open and there before me was a white horse, whose rider is called Faithful and True. With justice he judges and wages war. His eyes are like blazing fire, and on his head are many crowns. He has a name written on him that no one knows but he himself. He is dressed in a robe dipped in blood, and his name is the Word of God. The armies of heaven were following him, riding on white horses and dressed in fine linen, white and clean. (Rev. 19:11–14)

He came first as the Lamb slaughtered for the world's sin. He will come again as the Lion—this time to clean house. Do not doubt this Warrior. Do not dismiss His roar. He will clean house. He will crush evil. And He will prevail.

What can we say to such things? Jesus is not only the King of kings and Lord of lords. He is the Hero of heroes. We love the heroes we do only because they were a little like Him. They are the shadows cast by that great Light. He is the Hero we have all been searching for all our lives, even if we didn't know it. All of our hero worship can now be properly focused on Him. So when Jesus asks us to love Him, He is not asking us to do something strange or weird. He is asking us to love Him with the same awe and admiration we have felt for all our other heroes.

It is this love that will call a man out on a new path, to leave behind the shadows and head toward that one Light. It is the path to becoming heroic himself.

CHAPTER 6

THE CALL
OF THE COACH

"A good coach can change a game.
A great coach can change a life."
—John Wooden

"Though He did what He could to help the
multitudes, He had to devote Himself primarily
to a few men, rather than the masses, in
order that the masses could at last be saved.
This was the genius of His strategy."
—Robert Coleman, *The Master Plan of Evangelism*

As Jesus was walking beside the Sea of
Galilee, he saw two brothers, Simon called
Peter and his brother Andrew. They were
casting a net into the lake, for they were
fishermen. "Come, follow me," Jesus said.
—Matthew 4:18–19

After years of teaching high school, it was still my
favorite way to be addressed by students. It wasn't
Mr. Delvaux. It wasn't Mr. D. It was one word: Coach.

Along with teaching, I had the privilege of coaching cross-country and track. The formal instruction
of the classroom gave way to the informal coaching of
the athletic field. It was an opportunity to connect to

young men, training them in the mechanics of running. I would teach sprinters how to relax to reach their max speed. I would work with relay teams on the intricacies of baton passing. I would set up intervals for the cross-country team, giving them times to hit. In all of this, I would teach the why as well as the how behind the training, so they could buy in to the workouts. We would delve into exercise physiology, anaerobic thresholds, and heart rate monitoring.

The sport of running has a unique quality about it. You are asked to expend yourself maximally over a spread of time so that nothing is left at the end. To do so, you have to push beyond pain thresholds. But to face the pain is to face the fear. I would ask my teams to dig down beyond what they thought possible, beyond the fear. Here is where coaching became less science and more art. It also became more joy. As I walked with their fear, I got to be a part of moving these boys into manhood.

One young runner new to cross-country wanted to talk to me in my classroom after a workout. It was the day before his first race. With halting words and downcast face, he finally blurted it out. He was scared. I was surprised at his candor. I then got to reassure him that every runner is scared. It's what you do with the fear that matters. It was a revelation to him that he wasn't alone. He walked out my door with his head up. He also ran well in that first race.

A miler I coached with tremendous potential became increasingly upset over his season. The more he trained, the worse he got. During one difficult interval session on the track, he could not finish and had to stop, throwing himself down on the side of the track in frustration. He pulled his knees toward him with both arms and bowed his head in despair. As I sat down beside him, he expressed through tears his confusion and disappointment. I encouraged him as best as I could, but I didn't understand his training woes myself. Soon afterward though, we realized that he was not getting enough caloric intake. A change in his diet began to change his season. His growing excitement mirrored mine as his times began to improve. He was reaching his potential.

There was the conversation with a young sprinter concerning his goals for the track season. We sat in two plastic chairs facing each other in the large meeting room at our annual spring camp. What was a normal discussion I had with every runner was difficult for him. He was a chronic stutterer. But the more he felt safe with me in the conversation, the more I saw his stuttering subside. Over the season, I grew to love him and his heart to compete. So did the rest of the team.

There was the jumper who would explode in anger over his technical mistakes. He had recently lost his father to a heart attack, and I was able to speak to him about anger and grief. What he needed at that moment was not high jump drills. He needed to be hugged.

I have countless other stories like these. The wonder I felt in all of them was the wonder of being a coach. I was able to mentor these young men, being present and speaking into their hearts. If you've ever been a coach, you know what I mean. Everywhere you turn is wet cement. Everywhere you step, you leave footprints. I am still awed by the privilege.

LONGING FOR A COACH

The wet cement is there because every young man longs to be coached. The fragile stalk of masculinity sprouting up needs the attention and affirmation of a coach. Sometimes it can be his father. At other times, it's another man who comes for him. The coach fills that longing for a heroic mentor, a wise man he can follow. He longs for a guide through the mystery and turmoil of entering manhood. Without one, he gets lost—or gives up altogether.

This is why the experience of being uncoached is so heartbreaking for a young man. So much rage, depression, and self-destructive behavior finds its roots here. It was my central wound, one infused with so much pain that I couldn't speak about it for years. The few men in my life then were anything but mentors. I flinched in their presence. There was the nervous piano teacher who smoked one cigarette after another, held in his yellowing hands. There was the church youth adviser, a stolid man, whose comments were bizarre or confusing, often both. I have already told the story with my father. When his anxiety became anger, I felt afraid. It was just better to stay out of his way. I know now there were a few men who tried to reach into my life, such as the English teacher who encouraged me in my music and involved me in his theatrical productions. But I was so used to shutting men out by that time to staunch the wound that I blew him off.

Because of the lack of coaching, fear became my defining emotion, one that caused immense shame. I was fearful of pursuing girls, fearful of trying football, fearful of speaking my mind—anything that smacked of risk and failure I kept at a distance. But entering risk is how a boy enters manhood. So I remained stuck at fourteen, stillborn as a man. Behind the stuckness was the lie: *I am unworthy of being coached. There is nothing special about me. I am uncoachable.* With no one to pull me up and out, I retracted into myself to survive. The stinging pain of such a lie can scarcely be described. I have listened to so many men tell similar stories. They are the abandoned men, the uncoached men. One of my motivations for becoming a coach was to do something positive with the wound. The pain became the passion. I didn't want any young man to walk through the same wasteland.

COACHING IN THE GREAT STORIES

The necessity of a coach is also echoed in the great heroic tales. Every hero starts his journey with a coach, an older man whose wisdom prepares him for challenges ahead. Jean Valjean had his priest. Frodo had his Gandalf. Luke Skywalker had his Yoda. No modern film portrays the power of a coach perhaps better than *The Matrix.* It is the story of Mr. Anderson, a computer geek who lives in wretched anonymity. All his life, he has felt that something is wrong with the world. Little does he know that his world is a computer-generated image that does not exist. Human beings are actually enslaved, operating as batteries to power the life of artificially intelligent machines that have taken over the world. These machines have created the Matrix, an artificial world to keep mankind deceived and in bondage. Through the help of his coach Morpheus, Mr. Anderson begins to understand what is wrong with his world. He also begins to hear about his true identity. He is not a nobody. He is Neo, the New Man, the one who would free mankind. But first, he needs to be trained for his mission.

Morpheus coaches him through the complexities of kung fu fighting in a holographic world, correcting his mistakes and misunderstandings. He also teaches him about the enemy agents who roam the Matrix world, crushing any potential opposition. Most importantly, he calls him by his true name. He challenges Neo to see himself as more than what he thought, encouraging him to walk through the door Morpheus was opening for him. It is only in the climactic final fight scene where he does. As he owns his true name, he beats the agents at their own game. Without Morpheus, Neo would have never had a chance. He would have never known there was a door. Only with a coach could he find his identity and his quest.

When we turn to the greatest of all stories, we find the same pattern. The Son was coached by the Father. In answering His critics after healing a paralyzed man, Jesus simply referred them to His Father: "Very truly I tell you, the Son can do nothing by himself; he can do only what he sees his Father doing, because whatever the Father does the Son also does. For the Father loves the Son, and shows him all he does" (John 5:19–20). Did you catch that? The Son of God couldn't do a thing on His own. He had to be shown. He had to be taught. He had to be coached.

There is more here. Jesus is the great Hero of all time, but He is not bound to the patterns of our heroic myths. What He fulfills, He also supersedes. He is the Lord of story as well as history. This is nowhere more apparent than when we turn to the theme of coaching. The one Man whose life was supremely heroic is the one Man who wants to guide men into the same life. This is unprecedented in any heroic tale. The great Hero is also the great Coach.

Let's go back for a moment to our attempts at becoming heroic. They were, by and large, disasters. Our hope for nobleness degenerated into narcissism. Yet the desire remains. Could it be possible that Jesus knows our longing and wants us to become heroic like Him? It's not only possible, it's the whole point of Christianity. Jesus became like us so that we could become like Him. Paul puts it even more forcefully: God "predestined [us] to be conformed to the image of his Son" (Rom. 8:29). God's intention for us mirrors our longing. It seems He has written His hopes for us in our deepest desires.

There is even more. Jesus not only knows our longing to be heroic but also understands our desire for a coach. And He wants to personally coach us into that heroic life.

I know this whole line of thinking raises all sorts of objections: "But He was Jesus. I'm just a sinner." "I've never had a flesh-and-blood man to show me the way. That's what I need. How can He coach me if He's not physically present?" "I feel Jesus is so disappointed with me. I've made such a mess of things. How could He want that for me?" "I understand what you are saying, but I feel disconnected from Jesus, sometimes afraid of Him, sometimes ashamed of Him." You may have other objections. But notice the tenor of them all. They are all voicing the same ache. It's the ache of abandoned men, of uncoached men.

HOW JESUS COACHED MEN

Rather than answer the objections, I want to hone in on the ache. Let's do that by going to the New Testament Gospels. How did Jesus coach men? How did He come to them in the Gospels? He didn't start with a lecture. He didn't begin with handing out books. He didn't draw up a list of expectations. He started with a call: "Come, follow me" (Matt. 4:19). It was the call of the Coach. It was the call for men to come and just be with Him. He did this primarily for twelve men, ones who had little to offer: blue-collar fishermen, a seedy tax collector, a political insurgent, and others—all untutored men scorned by religious leaders. They were the abandoned men, the uncoached men. He came for them, and He called them. And what He did with them breaks all boundaries of the possible. With His coaching, they became bearers of the Kingdom, ushering in a new existence on earth. Whole books have been written on the genius of Jesus as a maker of men. He *was* the great Coach. Let's watch Him in action with Levi, also known as Matthew.

As Jesus was walking by the Sea of Galilee one day to head back into Capernaum, he ran across a tax collector's tollbooth owned by Levi (Mark 2:14–15). Tax collectors could levy a tax on anyone entering Capernaum from neighboring territories. But the tax system was set up to encourage flagrant greed and oppression. The city or district was leased out to the tax collector at a fixed sum by the governor, the hated Herod. The actual tax, though, was left up to the collector to charge, prompting exorbitant fees to profit the collector. Tax collectors were so despised that they were disqualified from being a judge or a witness in court. They were excommunicated from the local synagogue, and their families were held in disgrace. If anyone was an abandoned man, it was Levi.

Imagine him for a minute as an outcast, encountering hatred everywhere he went. Imagine everyone avoiding him, the cold eyes on his face and the whispers behind his back. Imagine how lonely he may have felt underneath the coldness of his greed.

Enter Jesus. He walked by Levi's workstation one day with a simple pronouncement. It was the call of the coach: "Follow me." Or literally, "Come after me." The phrase "after me" was a technical way of describing what a man did with a rabbi at that time. It meant that he was submitting himself to that rabbi to be his student. Following rabbis wasn't unusual then. What was unusual is how Jesus did it. Most students sought out a rabbi and then asked permission to follow. But Jesus took the initiative, summoning His disciples as a military officer would command His troops. It is likely that Levi had already heard Jesus teach and seen Him heal in Capernaum, but the text doesn't say for sure. As Jesus called him, Levi may have felt the power of His authoritative voice. He may have felt Jesus reaching in and touching that core sense of abandonment. We don't know for sure. What we do know is that He got up and followed. He left his corrupt life to come after Jesus.

The story doesn't end there. Levi, probably overcome with joy at being invited by Jesus to be with Him, wanted his friends to meet this amazing man. What kind of friends would ever hang out with Levi when he wasn't working? Other tax collectors, of course. So Levi throws a dinner party for Jesus at his home with his fellow collectors. They were all abandoned men, all uncoached men. And they all loved Jesus. They felt He was coming for them and enjoyed their company.

It is also important to remember that in those days eating together wasn't just a social occasion. Even today, in a world of fast-food eating, to be invited into someone's home for dinner is something special. Back then the feeling was heightened. To eat with a man was an expression of closeness to him. This sense of connection was further enhanced when we remember that the custom then was not to sit in chairs around a dinner table. They lay on couches. Those who ate together reclined with each other, something akin to lounging on a sofa together. Levi not only felt called by Jesus. He felt close to Him.

I also love the story of how Jesus first interacted with two of his future disciples (John 1:35–39). Both of them had been drawn to John the Baptist, perhaps believing he was a great prophet or the Messiah himself. He was certainly a hero to them. But after hearing John's words about Jesus one day and seeing Jesus themselves, their focus shifted. They wanted to see more. They wanted to hear more. So they tagged along behind Him, probably at some distance out of fear or awkwardness. Suddenly Jesus turned and asked them point-blank: "What do you want?" (v. 37). They must have been caught off guard by such directness. What did they want after all? A peek at greatness? A taste of His teaching? A chance to see a miracle? They probably weren't even sure what they wanted. So instead of giving an answer, they respond obliquely with another question, changing the subject: "Rabbi, where are you staying?" (v. 37). Jesus didn't scold them for their indirectness or demand an answer to His question. He didn't even give directions. He simply said, "Come, and you will see" (v. 39). I love that. I just love that. That's all they needed. It's all they really wanted. It was an invitation to come close to the Coach. The text says they responded to His call and came, spending the whole day with Him (v. 39).

TAGGING ALONG WITH THE HERO

Think back to one of your heroes. It may have been a great athlete, a famous musician, an acclaimed author, a winsome teacher, or a beloved coach. Then imagine how you might have felt if he had invited you to come and be with him for a day, tagging along with him in his daily activities. You would have felt astonished at such an offer and then honored that you had been singled out. But there is more to this invitation than you first realize.

Imagine that your hero not only invites you into his company but also offers to train you in his craft, in the very thing that made him seem so heroic to you, be it football or songwriting. He wants you to experience what he has experienced. He wants to open a door for you so that you can share in his greatness and taste it for yourself.

However unrealistic such a scenario sounds, this is exactly what Jesus did for His disciples. He spent three years, training and teaching them in the ways of the Kingdom. He wanted them to share in His greatness and glory. He wanted them to know the joy of becoming like Him. He opened a door that they could have never found on their own.

But Jesus is the same yesterday, today, and tomorrow. The Coach of the ages calls men to come and tag along beside Him so that He can rub off onto them. The great Hero wants to train men today in the ways of the heroic.

The fact that He is no longer present in body can seem like such a stumbling block to all of this. It wasn't that way to Jesus. In fact, He told His twelve men right before His death that it was better if He left. How could that be? He explains it this way: "And I will ask the Father, and he will give you another advocate to help you and be with you forever—the Spirit of truth" (John 14:16–17). If the Holy Spirit is another advocate, Jesus is implying that He is the first one. *Advocate* is a translation of the Greek word *paraclete*, a term used by the Greeks for someone called to come alongside and help as a legal counsel for the defendant. But the word *paraclete* carries other nuances difficult to translate into English. Those nuances come clearer when we think about Jesus as a *paraclete* for His twelve men. What did He do for them? He loved them, taught them, and guided them into the life of the Kingdom. Then He trained them by sending them out to practice what they had learned so that the Kingdom could spread to others. Finally, as He is about to depart, He informs them that a second *paraclete* is coming, to do for them what He did: "But the Advocate, the Holy Spirit, whom the Father will send in my name, will teach you all things and will remind you of everything I have said to you" (John 14:26). And this: "But when he, the Spirit of truth, comes, he will guide you into all the truth" (John 16:13). Jesus taught them and guided them. He coached them. His Holy Spirit will do that for us today.

STORIES OF PERSONAL COACHING

The reality of this is best explained through personal story. What happens when you receive Jesus' personal coaching through the Holy Spirit? It is coaching born out of an intimate knowledge of your story—your wounds and your joys, your questions and your hopes. It comes directed to you, with what you need for that moment. Remember, He knows you better than you know yourself. He can reach in and touch you at your core. The last fifteen years for me have been the adventure of learning to receive that personal coaching.

It often happens in the early morning silence on my back porch. As I attend to His Word and pray, I also listen for His coaching. It comes in many ways, but most often as the gentle voice of encouragement: "Let Me love you." "Rest in Me." "I am with you." Sometimes it is firmer: "Let Me heal you in My own time." "Fix your eyes on Me." "You will have to let Me guide you." At other times it comes as a statement or question to ponder: "I know your wound." "The only way to stay with Me is to stay inside yourself." "Will you serve others?" But sometimes the coaching is more pointed.

Once while on the porch, an image came up of myself at thirteen. I could see my thick glasses, my awkward demeanor, my crippling shame. Then I heard this: "I love to coach boys like you." It completely undid me. I wept. For the first time, I was able to see myself through His eyes. He saw me as one of the abandoned boys, the uncoached boys. It was for boys like me that He came.

But it's not just me. I have had the privilege of teaching other men to receive His coaching. Once while helping a man sort out his life quietly before the Lord, I asked him, "What might the Lord's invitation be to you right now?" Before he had a chance to ponder an answer, he heard a quiet inner voice: "Come rest in Me." He was so surprised. It was exactly what he needed as he faced growing demands at work and critical decisions about the future.

Another man I knew felt increasingly anxious over difficulties with an adult son. As we sat together in the silence to listen to the Lord, an image came to him. Wielding a pickax, he was trying to break up ground that was baked dry and hard. The labor was taxing. A few feet away, there was lush growth with a stream of water running through it. He was enticed by the sound of the water. Then He heard the Lord: "There's water over here you could take and pour on that land. Better yet, why don't you put down the ax and come to the water yourself?" It was an invitation to quit trying to do work that was not his. It was an invitation to allow the Lord to do the work in that son.

I have countless stories like these two. I believe Jesus is always seeking to coach us, but we don't take the time to listen or don't know how. The best place for both is the silence. It's where we let Scripture soak in us and voice our prayer. But most important, it's where we receive His coaching for the day. We are no longer the abandoned men, the uncoached men.

We are His men.

CHAPTER 7

INITIATION
BY DEATH

*"We want to reach the kingdom of God, but
we don't want to travel by way of death. And
yet there stands Necessity saying: 'This way,
please.' Do not hesitate, man, to go this way,
when this is the way that God came to you."*
—Augustine, "Exposition II, Sermon I on Psalm 30" in
Expositions on the Book of Psalms

*"He did not know that the new life would not
be given him for nothing, that he would have to
pay dearly for it, that it would cost him great
striving, great suffering. But that is the beginning
of a new story—the story of the gradual renewal
of a man, the story of his gradual regeneration,
of his passing from one world into another,
of his initiation into a new unknown life."*
—Fyodor Dostoyevsky, *Crime and Punishment*

*We always carry around in our body the death of
Jesus, so that the life of Jesus may also be revealed
in our body. For we who are alive are always
being given over to death for Jesus' sake, so that
his life may also be revealed in our mortal body.*
—2 Corinthians 4:10–11

To be initiated is to enter something you have never experienced. It requires facing fear and the unknown—even

facing death. It's how we grow as men. It's how we become men.

One of my most memorable initiations happened when I entered the world of off-trail hiking. As a lifelong backpacker, I have always loved reading maps and negotiating trails, but had never experienced life off of the trail. It happened while backpacking in the Rockies with a group of men. We had base-camped at well over ten thousand feet and had planned to hike each day up onto the mountain ridges and peaks. After a failed attempt to summit one day due to deep snowpack, we decided to descend off-trail with a GPS rather than backtrack the same trail. The consensus was that it would be more of an adventure. But as I eyed the massive boulder field that began our descent, I could feel my anxiety rising. It only accelerated when I realized that the steepness of the descent meant there would be no turning around. Once we started, we were committed. Even our robust leader soon became anxious. Eyeing a route through the maze of rocks, he planted his weight on one that looked stable. Instead, it wobbled and nearly sent him tumbling down. Injury up in this remote area would be perilous. For the next thirty minutes, all talking ceased as we gingerly picked our way through the talus field, setting our sights on a small alpine lake many hundreds of feet below. Each rock had to be tested. Each foot plant had to be checked. One false move could send us hurtling down the boulder field or start a rockslide onto the others. You could feel the tension in the silence.

Even after making it to the lake and regathering our strength, plenty of obstacles remained. There were snow banks to slide down, steep embankments to negotiate, and waterfalls to maneuver around—all without a visible trail. At each turn, I dreaded meeting an impassable obstacle. Yet I was also able to rise above my fear at moments. It was then that I realized we were going where few had ever gone, seeing what few had ever seen. There was eerie beauty in the azure blueness of the lakes, in the endless expanse of serrated peaks, and in the silence of the lush undergrowth. I marveled at the wonders surrounding me as the trail continued to descend. In the midst of my quiet reverie, we suddenly spied the lake nearest our base camp. We had made it! Relief surged up through me. We celebrated by plunging into the frigid waters of that lake. But along with the relief, something new had been etched into me. I had been initiated into off-trail hiking. I had faced the fear and walked through it. I went out that morning as one man. I came back as another.

I have felt this same initiation process on countless occasions. There was the time I entered the world of road biking, learning to clip in, shift gears, and change a flat. But my real initiation happened in a draft line as we screamed down an enormous hill reaching speeds over 40 mph. If I left the line to slow down, I could wobble and fall. If I stayed, I would keep accelerating until the road leveled. Holding my place in that line felt like death, but I chose to face the fear and hold. As we came to the end of the hill and slowed, I felt the same relief and the same etching. I came back from that ride different than when I began.

I felt the initiation again as I learned to manage a 4-wheeler over rock-strewn paths and up impossibly steep passageways. It happened as I summited my first mountain more than fourteen thousand feet, trembling with fatigue and joy. It happened as I planted my first kiss, preached my first sermon, and skydived my first time. Each time I had to face the fear. Each time I had to push through it. Each time I walked away knowing that something had shifted inside. I would not go back to what I once was.

MALE INITIATION

The etching and shifting is all part of becoming a man. We fear initiation. Yet we long for it as well. Something primal in our souls urges us: "This is the way." We must be thrust into death before we can attain life. My first clue to the universality of this urging happened at the annual camp for my cross-country team. These young men would spend five days together at a state park—running, biking, and swimming each day. It would all climax in a mini-triathlon. They would tell me that the camp was the hardest thing they had ever done. Then they couldn't wait to come back next year. It took me a long time to figure out the contradiction between these two statements. The camp had become an initiation for them into the world of physical endurance. They had been tested and came back as different young men.

Male initiation rites have been a part of primitive cultures from time immemorial. It could have been killing a bear, going without food or water, or enduring some physical wound. Each culture seemed to have its own unique way of doing it. The initiation was answering the call planted in the male psyche: there is a need to face pain, fear, and death. That call still beckons men today. We cannot just walk into manhood. We must fight and risk to enter it. However much we may fear the testing, we fear being left untested even more.

Much of the male angst and anger today comes from this brooding sense of being uninitiated. I saw this firsthand with the high school young men I taught for years. There are now few rites left in our culture to benchmark any sense of entering manhood: getting a driver's license, getting drunk, having sex. But those rites are pitifully insufficient. They leave young men more confused than ever. There is no coaching from mentors, no community of men around them, and no celebration of the benchmark. They walk into college and the work world unfinished—with the bodies of men and the souls of boys.

INITIATION IN STORY

The need for initiation comes out in all the great stories as well. Part of the heroic journey in literature always involves the trials a hero faces, culminating in a final ordeal. He must persevere through them and even let his life go to complete the quest. In the process, he is initiated into a new life—the life of the heroic—where he can use what he has gained for the good of others. Think about our hero Maximus for a minute. He faces constant death as a gladiator, yet must fight his enemy

Commodus in a final ordeal while badly wounded. He manages to kill Commodus, but dies himself as well. Only then could his quest succeed of getting revenge and restoring justice to Rome.

In *Star Wars*, Luke Skywalker faces his final ordeal by attempting to destroy the Death Star. The survival of the Rebel Alliance depends on the success of his venture. After watching several of his fighter pilots die in the attempt, he chooses to trust the Force rather than rely on his own strength. That choice to let go and trust in the face of death ends with the Death Star being blown up. Luke comes back a true hero.

Frodo faces continual trials as he journeys to Mordor to destroy the ring: skirmishes with the enemy and conflicts among his own companions. The final ordeal happens when he cannot let go of the ring inside of Mount Doom. Gollum then unexpectedly appears and bites off his finger to obtain the ring. But Gollum loses his balance and falls into the bowels of the mountain, perishing along with the ring. Frodo has completed his quest but is marked forever without a finger. He has saved the Shire and Middle Earth and is celebrated as a hero.

Think about any story with a hero you love. At some point, he has to face fear. He has to face death. And he has to choose to let himself go. It is in that choice that he becomes heroic. Something shifts inside. Something is etched in him forever. He starts his quest out as one man. He comes back as another. He has been initiated by death. Ironically, it's also the path into life.

My own desire to be initiated and take a heroic journey always surfaced in these stories. The longing would rise and peak, overwhelming me like the tide. But as I closed the book or put the DVD away, it would soon ebb and fade. I was set back into my ordinary world, one of feeling uninitiated as a man. My only recourse was to keep escaping into story, so I could feel the thrill of the heroic vicariously. It wasn't the real thing, but at least I felt something pulsating with life. Yet, I was still on the outside of it, longing to enter, but not knowing how.

INITIATION AND JESUS

My confusion only deepened when I considered Jesus. For many years, I couldn't understand why He never spoke about initiation. I wondered if His ways were somehow lacking. Perhaps He didn't really understand the heart of a man. Perhaps I would have to look elsewhere to become a man.

One day as I was pondering these things, it hit me like a thunderclap. What Jesus offered was, in fact, initiation—of the most universal breadth and in the highest, most complete way. It surpasses any initiation rite. It supersedes any heroic story. He is the new Adam, the new Man whose likeness we are to bear, and He wants to unleash that new Adam inside each of us. He does this through the initiatory rite of baptism. It is a symbol for the washing away of our sin—all of our warped attempts at heroic status, all of our narcissism and petty jealousy. But it also symbolizes death. In ancient times, most men did not know how to swim, so being in water, especially deep water, was feared. It was an abyss associated with death. To be baptized was to be taken down into those waters of death so that we could rise into the life of Christ. Paul makes this point clear in Romans: "We were therefore buried with him through baptism into death in order that, just as Christ was raised from the dead through the glory of the Father, we too may live a new life" (6:4).

But what does it look like to live this? What is it like to feel that we are buried with Christ so that we can rise with Him? Jesus makes this reality clear in one of His well-known pronouncements. Yes, He will ask us to face the fear. Yes, He will ask us to face the unknown. He will also ask us to face death: "Whoever wants to be my disciple must deny themselves and take up their cross and follow me" (Mark 8:34).

A little explanation is in order. To deny yourself is not to hate yourself. Nor is it an attempt at self-annihilation so that only Christ remains. Such maneuvers inevitably fail, only drawing you back into more self-preoccupation. Instead, to deny yourself is to refuse any more attempts at being your own hero. It is to let go of your agendas for fame, power, and success. It is a radical shift in the gravitational center of a man's soul. We move from the narcissist to a noble man only by this reckless abandonment to God's will. The idea of self-denial is then reinforced by the image of a death march. To take up the cross was to carry your own cross beam on the way to your death by crucifixion. The image would have jarred His listeners. It was meant to. This initiation cuts deeper than any other ever prescribed.

But the point of self-denial and self-execution is not death alone. The point is to do this so that we can follow

Jesus. All great leaders go first and then ask others to follow. Jesus is no exception. Where the great Hero has gone is where the great Coach will ask us to follow. He is not doing this to kill us. He's doing this to make us into men. His supremely heroic life led Him through the horror of the cross and into the wonder of the resurrection. To become like that great Hero is to walk the same path. Really, should we be surprised? Haven't all the heroic stories prepared us for this? Haven't all our longings for initiation told us of the need to face fear and death?

Jesus then adds a reinforcing statement, this time explaining the tragedy of not choosing the heroic route: "For whoever wants to save their life will lose it, but whoever loses their life for me and for the gospel will save it" (v. 35). If a man focuses on preserving his life, continuing to write his own story of winning, status-seeking, and climbing to the top, he will lose it all in the end. There will be collapse, ruin, and loss. It's the old chase for false glory. I know too many men whose stories have ended this way. You do too. But if a man chooses to let his life go because of Jesus, if he chooses what all heroes at some point must choose, he has begun to step into the heroic life. In this letting go, he will come out on the other side a different man. Something will be forever etched into him. Something will have forever shifted.

The new Adam is being unleashed.

ENTERING DEATH

There is more here to persuade us that this is the right path. The idea of discovering life by tasting death is a paradox built into the fabric of the universe. We see it in the agonizing labor a mother experiences, ending with a new life. We see it in our expanding emotional bandwidth as grief opens up new doorways of joy. We see it in the cocoons of moths, in the changes of the seasons, in the buried seeds that sprout forth as new plants. However much these analogues may help us accept the paradox, that's not the point. The point is to enter death ourselves. The point is to trust and go.

I have found no better place to experience this on a physical level than at the gym I visit each week. The workouts are posted on a white board, each one seeking to improve strength, mobility, and aerobic conditioning. My coach is a young man named Sean, who constructs the workouts with a level of mastery and creativity. In all the time I have gone there, I have never done the same one twice. After prepping a group of us on the day's routine, he then keeps his eye on us as we start, correcting mistakes and encouraging us along. Sean and I have come up with a phrase for the conditioning piece. We call it "descending into the abyss." The level of aerobic distress you encounter at times is unnerving. It feels like death.

Recently I was working through a conditioning sequence, alternating intervals on the stationary bike with planks. At the halfway mark, I already wondered if I could finish. I panicked for a moment as the oxygen I sucked down didn't seem to be enough for my racing heart. Would I pass out? I continued to scrape along the bottom of the abyss through the second half of the sequence, willing myself to the end. I fell to the ground in a heap, exhausted. It was painful. It was ugly. But I came back that week for more. The reason is what happens after each workout. I feel vigorous and alive with improving strength and mobility. Another reason is not so obvious. Sean constructs these workouts and does them first himself to make sure we can do them. He has descended into the abyss and knows that we will come out of it. I have learned to trust him.

This is as good a picture as I know of for the death Jesus calls us to enter. Descending into the abyss of death is how we become men, radiating the heroic life. Still we may hesitate. And for good reason. There is nothing attractive about death. It looks ugly. It feels ugly. It is ugly. So we shrink back and doubt: *This is where Jesus is taking me? Really? Isn't there another way into the heroic that's a little less dramatic, a little less shocking? Isn't there a more sensible route into this new man?* We may then avoid and dismiss, only to come back around that there is no other way. Even then, we may continue to analyze the situation, hoping this will stall the inevitable. This is the fear in all initiation. We are being called into something we have not known. We are being formed into someone we have not been. The unknowns are gaping. It feels perilous.

There is one realization that can help us. We can trust Jesus with this route because He traversed the same one. He entered a death that no one had ever known, crushed by our sin and shame. He descended into the abyss and came up out of it, dripping with glory. He pioneered the route into the new Adam, doing the impossible thing we couldn't. Now He asks us to follow, to trust Him and to enter. He knows the abyss, and He knows we will come out of it more alive than ever.

How Jesus asks us to die will take on a different complexion in each man's story. But do not doubt it. He will always lead you here. I was faced with such a choice at the beginning of the ministry I now lead. My time as a high school Bible teacher and coach had been one of tremendous affirmation. God began to do much healing in my life as I offered that same healing to students. But toward the end of that twenty-year stint, I knew He was stirring new things in me. I had begun to work with men in classes and small groups and realized that this was the new trajectory I was to take. For the next three years, I tried to make a smooth transition so that I could work with both students in the school and men in the church. All efforts failed. The only way forward was to start something new. I shrunk back in fear. The financial risks were perilous. The emotional ones were worse. The possibility of failure loomed large. This was too much. Surely there must be another way. But none appeared. I was being asked to enter death. I was being asked to trust and go.

Only with the urging of friends was I able to make the jump. But it did not lead to instant life. It really was a jump into death. There were so many times I wanted to give up during those first three years. There were events that were cancelled and opportunities that didn't materialize. The shame of failure followed me like an unwanted shadow. Then there were the anxiety attacks brought on by financial stress. There was even a time of depression when I felt the darkness closing in around me. The falling continued as deeper issues of identity surfaced. I had defined myself as a teacher and a coach for years. Without these, who was I anymore? I had no answer. Throughout all of this, I continually heard Jesus whisper to me: "Follow Me. Walk with Me. Trust Me." The words were a continual reassurance that this was the right way even though it felt like death. Where was all this going? How would it end? There was no answer. Only a call to trust and keep going.

But through it all, there was a discernable shift in my soul. I was being called into something I did not know. I was being formed into someone I had not been. The old narcissist in me was dying. Something new was being birthed. I was no longer on the outside reading stories or watching movies of men on their heroic journeys. I had entered. I was on one myself. I felt it distinctly during the fourth year of the ministry as I began to lay down the framework for this book. I had walked through the gauntlet of fear, anxiety, and failure and had come out on the other side.

I had entered death—only to find life.

A FINAL IMAGE

One of the most gripping images of finding life in death comes from the pen of the Scottish myth writer, George MacDonald. His fairy tale *Lilith* chronicles the journey of a man entering an alternate reality through an enchanted attic mirror. In this fairy tale land, he will discover his identity and his quest, but first he is asked to enter death. Near the beginning of the tale, he is taken into a massive underground room by a strange sexton and his wife. The room is filled with couches on which lay those who have died, each covered with a thin white sheet. It is deathly cold and quiet, yet the atmosphere is not grotesque. Instead, there is a hushed peace in the chill. He is told that all of these have fallen asleep and wait being awakened. Then he is shown his own couch. The choice is now before him: Should he lie down or run away? Trembling, he asks questions to delay the decision. Finally the sexton turns to him and says: "Do not be a coward . . . Turn your back on fear, and your face to whatever may come. Give yourself up to the night, and you will rest indeed. Harm will not come to you, but a good you cannot know."[8] He cannot do it. He refuses and flees.

Toward the end of the story, after many trials and adventures, he returns to the underground cemetery, repentant and ready with these words: "Will you not pardon both my cowardice and my self-confidence, and take me in? I give myself up. I am sick of myself and wish to sleep the sleep."[9] He now understands. Only by entering death can he come alive. He goes to his couch and throws himself on it. The death he once refused is now the death he longs for.

We only long for this kind of death when we become sick of ourselves and desperate for initiation as men. We are then ready to enter. But through what kind of death will Jesus take us? Where will He lead us? That answer forms the substance of the next two chapters.

CHAPTER 8

DETACHING

*"Every one of us is, even from his mother's
womb, a master craftsman of idols."*
—John Calvin, *Commentary on the Acts
of the Apostles*

*"Love may forgive all infirmities and
love still in spite of them: but Love
cannot cease to will their removal."*
—C. S. Lewis, *The Problem of Pain*

*What agreement is there between the temple
of God and idols? For we are the temple of
the living God. As God has said: "I will live
with them and walk among them, and I will
be their God, and they will be my people."*
—2 Corinthians 6:16

I met Alan as a student in one of my night classes. He
was a likeable young man in his twenties with a winsome smile and an engaging personality, but behind that
exterior warmth lay a story of chilling darkness. As he
shared bits of it during the class, I found out that he was
helping to manage a halfway house for detoxed addicts
trying to reenter normative life. He was a former drug
addict himself. As messy as that story seemed, the real
chaos came much earlier.

It began with an alcoholic, bipolar mother. There were peaceful days with her as a good mom, interrupted by physical beatings and accusations. Alan's dad left her when Alan was six, only to be followed by a stepfather who also ended up being an alcoholic. He took out his rage on Alan and his mom by beating both of them. Then there was Alan's introduction into pornography at nine years of age when his stepdad forced him to view it. When the stepdad finally left, his mom developed schizophrenia, losing touch with reality and beating Alan mercilessly, one time leaving him bloodied and bruised on the side of the road.

His only escape from such chaos was sports. During his boyhood, he was a phenomenal tennis player. That natural athletic talent showed up later in his dominant ability on the baseball field in high school. Here he found some measure of success and affirmation. Then his grandfather, a caring and stable man, seemed to provide another escape. He finally got custody of Alan and brought him into a safe home. But it wasn't enough to undo the tangled mess of his childhood. The rules and structure felt confining, and Alan started to rebel. He discovered his new love—alcohol. The excessive drinking provided immediate relief and escape.

Then more chaos followed. Alan had already experienced profound disappointment with the men in his life. His real father had abandoned him and his stepfather had abused him. The pattern of disappointment repeated itself with his baseball coach, who at first initiated a strong relationship with him. Alan loved the attention of an older male, but the interest soon felt constricting, as the coach demanded more of his personal time. He finally stopped playing baseball, only to find out afterwards that the coach had been charged with fifty counts of sexual abuse to other young men. Alan had escaped that trauma, but the experience cemented his belief that no man could ever be trusted. That belief led to more chaos.

He began to steal from his grandparents and neighbors. He turned to gambling and pornography. The descent continued as he dropped out of college, became homeless, and turned to heroin, his life now circling around crack dealers and prostitutes. He had dropped to the bottom of the pit and faced thoughts of suicide. What saved him was a call of desperation to his aunt asking for help. It started his journey into recovery.

That recovery involved ceasing all the addictions. As he stopped, what surfaced was an unquenched longing for male relationships. So he made the courageous step to start trusting men again. He now talks to his grandfather daily on the phone as well as his sponsor. He's working on his college degree, receiving managerial training at his job, and going to church regularly. He knows his calling in life is to help others, whether it's as a counselor or a minister.

Looking back, Alan now knows that all of his addictions only hardened his heart. He could only look at life through a tightly narrowed perspective, like a tiny peephole in a door. As he has let those addictions go, the whole door has opened. His hardened heart has opened as well to God and to others. Alan summarizes his story this way: "When I let gambling, women, and porn go, I could see God showing up more. The way I feel acceptance now is different. It's pure."

Alan's story is exceptional in the chaos he experienced. But the patterns of his story are universal. Every man attaches to something hoping to find life. Instead, it destroys him.

THE POWER OF ATTACHMENT

As infants, we come into this world yearning to attach. Our emotional and cognitive frameworks can never be self-constructed. It comes as we interact and attach to those who care for us, primarily our parents. We download their responses to us, and that download becomes the interpretative grid through which we perceive the world and ourselves in it. Or course, all of this happens long before we can put words to it. Yet it happens nonetheless. This molding of our inner world then solidifies as we move into adolescence and manhood. Our way of attaching to our parents, especially our fathers, now becomes our way of being as men. Here lies the tragedy of so many sons with their fathers. If the attachment formed was not engaging or affirming, if it was violent or silent, a son will push away from his father to self-protect, but the thirst to attach won't. That thirst will drive him to other things, to anything that will offer affirmation or stop the pain of disconnection. These become his disordered attachments, disordered because they put created things in place of the Creator, but disordered also because of the chaos they unleash in his soul. Psychologically, we call them addictions.

Theologically, we call them idols. Whatever their name, they become the tottering framework on which a man tries to build his life.

These disordered attachments now become absorbed into his self-constructed heroic story, one of achieving success, garnering fame, or amassing power. Conversely, they can also become his anesthetic against repeated failure, lurking obscurity, or crippling woundedness. They will give him just enough of a rush to keep him coming back for more, not knowing that he is sipping a soul-arsenic that will poison him. They will never make him noble. They will only bring chaos and ruin. It's every man's story. It's my story too.

My experience of disordered attachments could not be any different than Alan's. I came from a stable family. I have no history of alcohol or drug addiction. I have no story of physical abuse. Yet the underlying story line is eerily parallel. The silence of my father and the disappointment with other male figures left me isolated and disconnected from the masculine structure of the world. That unmet longing to attach was crystallized in a small vignette from my sophomore year in high school. It was a gray winter day, when the bone-crunching chill sucked all warmth out of me. It was only to be matched by the chill in my soul. Depression had become my unwanted companion. As I walked up the steps of a classroom building after school, something off to my right caught my eye, and I stopped to look. There on a playing field, I saw some of my classmates scrambling after a soccer ball in heated competition. The game had just been introduced into our area as an official sport. I saw the hustle, the laughter, the push-and-shove. I longed to join in and thought about the exhilaration it would bring. But only for a second. What came next was an internal sigh along with a familiar capitulation. I could never risk that. Through other shaming experiences in sports, I had already branded myself as unqualified. I could not expose myself to such failure again. I pushed the longing down as bitter tears rose up. I turned my face away from the soccer game and continued climbing the steps into the building. I was never to play on that field.

A lie already planted in my heart took a deeper rooting that day: *Sports is the gateway into the life you long for. Yet you are not worthy of entering.* That lie became the slow-acting arsenic I sipped on for years, poisoning me with a hyper-idealization of sports and a compulsion to enter. My unhealthy attachment to them later surfaced in a cyclical addiction to endurance running and excessive eating. It also became the energy behind my early years as a coach that nearly wrecked my marriage.

Other harmful attachments ensued during my years as a young man. There was the on-and-off flirtation with pornography. There was a compulsion to succeed and an avoidance of failure. There was an obsession with knowledge as a way of exhibiting intellectual power. Because I had no emotional download of healthy attachment, I scavenged for anything that provided some sense of strength and wisdom, anything that covered my weakness and ineptness. The maddening part was that I still clung to my attachments long after I understood how they were ruining me. But I knew no other option. My patterns of being had become ruts, seemingly incapable of shift or repair. My idols had become my oxygen. I had to have them.

I have listened to the stories of other men, all with the same eerie parallels. They are different in detail, but alike in result. We choose an idol, hoping to find life. Instead, we find death and lose even the power to choose.

THE DEATH GRIP OF IDOLS

The book of 1 John ends in a striking way: "Dear children, keep yourselves from idols" (5:21). I used to think this was such an odd way to end an epistle focused on the love and life Jesus gives. Not anymore. This was John's last word to his readers, one he wanted them to remember perhaps above all. If we don't keep ourselves from idols, they will ruin everything. If we don't focus on the love and life given through Jesus, we will turn to idols to find them.

The precedent for such a view is woven into the Old Testament story. So much of it deals with how the Israelites keep turning away from the living God to prostitute themselves before dead idols. In fact, the whole book of Judges portrays the death grip idolatry had on the Israelites. They keep turning to false gods even after God keeps rescuing them. It's not that they quit believing in God; it's that they didn't feel He was enough. Would He truly protect them and provide for them? Maybe He would. Maybe He wouldn't. The idea of unequivocal trust in a God they couldn't control seemed too risky. They wanted to be like the other nations whose

gods could be controlled through sacrifice and appease-
ment. So along with keeping the Lord as their God, they
added other gods as well. Even after those gods brought
ruin, the Israelites kept forsaking the Lord and turning
back to them. The idols had become their oxygen. They
had to have them.

It's easy to judge the Israelites for their foolishness.
Why couldn't they see that these idols were dead? Why
couldn't they see the death they brought? Why couldn't
they run away from the grip of idolatry? Now I know
better. We have all been foolish men, auctioning our
hearts off to idols, only to find that we cannot buy them
back. Once attached, we do not know how to detach.

A MYTHIC PARALLEL

One of the clearest images of this comes from the
character of Gollum in *Lord of the Rings*. He first
encounters the One Ring of power as Sméagol, a hobbit
with an inordinate desire to dig and tunnel, but more out
of curiosity rather than evil intent. One day he accom-
panies a friend on a fishing adventure to the Gladden
Fields. His friend snags a huge fish, is dragged out of
the boat, and comes up out of the water sputtering. He
has no fish but a mysterious ring that he has scooped
up from the bottom. Its evil power soon drives Sméagol
mad with lust, and he kills his friend to possess it, calling it "my precious." Because of the unnatural power the
ring gives him, his family shuns him and drives him out
of the Shire. He takes to being a cave creature, hiding
in the darkness, because the light of the sun begins to

hurt him. He hardly remembers his former life and lives alone, consumed by the ring. It gives Sméagol visions of power and control over others, but they are all lies. It is the ring who has power and control over Sméagol. Shrunken to a pathetic state, he is no longer Sméagol, but Gollum, because of the disgusting noise he makes in his throat. He loves and hates the ring, loves it for its power, yet hates it for the ruin it causes. Because he can't let it go, it slowly destroys him. In the end, it finally does, hurtling him into the churning lava of Mount Doom, still clutching the ring.

The story of Gollum's disordered attachment is a visceral parallel to our own. But it was never meant to be that way. Our fathers were meant to be living icons of God Himself. As growing boys, we were meant to attach to them, letting their masculine glory rub off onto us, as they nourished us in their protective love. That love was then to point us to the great Father Himself. As we grew into men, we were to attach to Him, loving Him and basking in His glory. But this scenario has been short-circuited from the beginning. Every man finds a ring, calls it "my precious," and sells his soul for it, hoping to become heroic. Instead it castrates him, emotionally and spiritually. Now emasculated, he is shrunken to a pathetic state. He hides from others. He forgets his name. And he can't let it go.

THE GRACE TO DETACH

When Jesus came, His message could be boiled down something like this: *The kingdom of God is near. The rescue of man is upon you. Forsake your disordered attachments and sins. Instead, follow Me. Attach to Me.* There is no better illustration of this message than His conversation with a wealthy man who was a spiritual seeker. He ran up to Jesus and flung himself down on his knees in humble deference. His question? He wanted to know what good works he had to accomplish to gain eternal life. Jesus responded by listing many of the Ten Commandments, shrewdly leaving out the tenth one that deals with coveting (Mark 10:17–19). When the man naively responded that he had obeyed them all from his youth, he was stunned by the response: "Jesus looked at him and loved him. 'One thing you lack,' he said. 'Go, sell everything you have and give to the poor, and you will have treasure in heaven. Then come, follow me'" (v. 20–21).

What Jesus says here is what He says to all of us. He is not berating the man for his covetousness, nor shaming him for wealth. Far from it. In the midst of this man's attachment to money, Jesus just loves him. But He loves him too much to leave him chained to his wealth. He calls him to detach from it. But the detachment is not meant to be a burden. It is both harsher and kinder, like ripping off a bandage from the skin quickly instead of in tiny pulls. Harsher because it is a call to give up what has defined this man. Kinder because Jesus is opening the door into a freedom that makes wealth pale in comparison. Jesus wants this man to follow Him, to attach to Him. But the detachment must come first. And here is the catch. It's the catch of every idol. How do we detach from something that has us in its grip?

The answer comes in the account. It's Jesus' love: "Jesus looked at him and loved him" (v. 21). Most addictions are driven by emptiness or shame. We must then keep returning to the idol to cover the escalating emptiness or shame that inevitably follow. Moralistic calls to stop only yield more desperation. We have lost our freedom to detach. But the chains are broken when we feel loved right there in our bondage. This is what Jesus did with this wealthy man. That love opened up the possibility to let go. But the choice was still his. Will he receive the love and detach? Sadly this story did not end well: "At this the man's face fell. He went away sad, because he had great wealth" (v. 22).

A modern retelling of this account comes from the story of young pastor addicted to pornography. Given the opportunity to speak to a church about fatherhood and sexual brokenness, he scolded the men with calls to forsake pornography. Then he turned around that evening and binged on it himself for hours. When his lust had spent itself, he sensed that God wanted to talk with him. Expecting nothing but rage from Him, he was surprised to see a vision of himself in prison with prison clothes on, going through the food line. He then sat at a table by himself to eat. Suddenly he saw Jesus coming over to sit down with him, also in prison clothes. After promising to eat with him whenever invited, Jesus suddenly said, "By the way, the door's open. You can leave anytime you want." What broke this man was not the open door or the invitation to leave. What broke him was the fact that Jesus was there with him, dressed as a prisoner, ready to eat with him. Jesus came to him in his bondage and loved him right there in the midst of his shame and degradation. It completely melted him in tears. It also gave him the power to detach and start the road to recovery.[10]

The grace to detach is just that. It's a grace given. The experience of being loved in our bondage is both the undoing of shame and the liberation from idols. It is the love that releases us to attach to Jesus, to love Him with all our hearts. At the same time, the grace given prompts a choice, one we now have the freedom to make. Will we receive the love and let go, or will we stay in our prison? Perhaps the first really heroic thing a man does is right here. It is an act of tremendous courage with a willingness to walk into the unknown. He chooses to enter the death of detachment. It is all part of his initiation.

Here is how that detachment happened with one of my idols. After decades of running, I ended up one day in the office of a hip doctor. The pain in my lower left back had increased to the point where I could no longer ignore it. Sitting on the side of the examining table, I was informed that I had minor hip arthritis. If I didn't stop running, I would face a hip replacement. I was stunned. My whole world had revolved around running. I was being asked to detach. It felt like I was dying. As I drove home from the doctor, I noticed a runner bolting down the shoulder of the road. A pang of grief shot through me. Running had become my identity. Who was I without it? But there was more to be abandoned. I had spent hours on long runs with my cross-country teams as they trained. It's where the good conversations happened. The thought of sending them out to run and staying behind left me cold. I knew I would have to give up coaching as well.

What happened next was unforeseen. After the decision to stop running, I woke up one morning feeling unburdened. I knew why. I didn't have to schedule my day around getting in the requisite run. I had time to take up new adventures. After saying good-bye to coaching, another surprise happened. The energy behind coaching—my longing to enter and connect through sports—surfaced. I had spent so long as a coach trying to answer the question of my worth as a man, but coaching never answered the question. Into that question, Jesus now came.

Early one morning, I was meditating on the mission of Jesus and on God's desire to bring all things under His Son's rule (Eph. 1:3–14). It was then that I heard Jesus' whisper, "Come be My brother." My heart leapt at the invitation. Unsolicited, something from the depths of my soul began to cry out loud, "I don't want to leave You. I don't want to leave You." It was the cry of a young man longing to attach, the desire I had pushed down that winter afternoon on the school steps to staunch the pain. This was how He would bring His rule into my life. This was how He was going to answer the question. He was going to help me feel worthy of the company of men. He would do that by inviting me into His company as a brother. It is not without wonder that I read in Hebrews: "Jesus is not ashamed to call [us] brothers" (2:11). There is no shame, no criticism—just the call to attach to Him as a brother. Along with the healing has come a freedom I didn't think possible. My heart is able to roam the terrain of masculinity, accepting a worth freely given. But there is more.

HEROIC FREEDOM

All of us construct our own heroic schemes to prove ourselves as men. I have already mentioned my recurrent dream to become a world-famous preacher. I have a good friend who kept envisioning himself as a rock star. Whether it's success, fame, or power, dreams like these dominate the landscape of our hearts, but in so doing they blot out the path to the truly heroic.

Think again about the real heroes you know in story or real life. It is precisely those dreams they gave up to do something else. They had found a cause greater than the outcome of their lives. In that discovery, they also stumbled upon the freedom to embrace whatever outcome came with the cause. Whether poverty or wealth, a short life or a long one, obscurity or acclaim—it didn't matter anymore.

This freedom from demanding a preconceived outcome to our lives can happen as we attach to the living Christ. It is the noble cause of His Kingdom to which we give ourselves. We begin to love Him more than we love our lives. The apostle Paul felt this heroic freedom. It was also the secret of his contentment: "I know what it is to be in need, and I know what it is to have plenty. I have learned the secret of being content in any and every situation, whether well fed or hungry, whether living in plenty or in want" (Phil. 4:12). Poverty or abundance were both acceptable to him as his heart burned for

Jesus. All the lives of the great saints through the ages tell the same tale. Entering the death of detachment gives us the freedom to live heroically.

But there is another death we must pass through on the heroic journey. Through that gauntlet, we now proceed.

CHAPTER 9

UNMASKING

*"The fear involved in shame is of permanent
abandonment, or exile. Those who see our
reprehensible core will be so disgusted and sickened
that we will be a leper and an outcast forever."*
—Dan Allender, *The Wounded Heart*

*"All sin starts from the assumption that my false
self, the self that exists only in my own egocentric
desires, is the fundamental reality of life to which
everything else in the universe is ordered."*
—Thomas Merton, *New Seeds of Contemplation*

*. . . put on the new self, created to be like
God in true righteousness and holiness.*
—Ephesians 4:24

I am always drawn to men who push through shame.
Their stories feel heroic. Their stories are heroic.

One such story is portrayed in the TV movie *The
Loneliest Runner*. The drama centers on a fourteen-
year-old boy who is a chronic bed wetter. His mother
punishes him by doing the unthinkable: she hangs his
yellowed sheets outside the front bedroom window for
everyone to see. He has to quit football, so he can sprint
home every day after school to pull the sheets out of the
window. This appalling scenario is not just a movie but

a true story as well. The screenplay writer drew from his own traumatic childhood, where his mother meted out the same punishment for his bed-wetting, hanging the sheets out for public display. To add to the tragedy, his issue was triggered by the enormous stress he felt over his fragile and suicidal mother. He once even had to rescue her from trying to drown herself. But he refused to let his shame define him, writing the script to publicly address the issue of bed-wetting. That was only after he had become a household name, starring in one successful TV series after another: *Bonanza*, *Little House on the Prairie*, and *Highway to Heaven*. Sadly, he contracted pancreatic cancer and died in his fifties, yet by that time, he had become heroic to so many. His name? Michael Landon.

Another true account of pushing through shame lies hidden in the records of England's royalty. Albert, the second son of King George V, was a stutterer. It was heartbreaking to hear him struggle to speak before crowds in his official duties as a prince. His childhood revealed only more heartbreak. Bertie, as he was called by his family, suffered from stomach issues, caused by a nurse's neglect when he was a baby. He also had knock-knees that were treated with painful splints. As a sickly boy, he developed a weak personality, given to shyness and crying. All of this brought on the stammer in his voice by the time he was eight. As such, he lived in the shadow of his older brother, David, who was athletic, handsome, and confident. But living behind his brother was an ironic blessing. He would not be the first in line to the throne and face the nightmare of being a king with a stutter.

For the stutterer, what seems most natural to everyone else becomes a point of repeated shame. Every conversation becomes a place of exposure. The worst nightmare of all is public speaking. That nightmare happened when Bertie's father, King George V, died and his brother, David, abdicated the throne to marry a divorced woman. He would now have to become the king. To add to his plight, war was looming with Hitler. With the help of a speech coach, however, Bertie found his voice as King George VI and helped lead England through the dark days of World War II. Historians describe his leadership and character as heroic.

That heroic life gripped the heart of a young boy named David Seidler, who left England as a refugee during World War II and grew up in America. He developed a stammer himself, probably due to the stresses of being a refugee. But as he listened to the wartime speeches of King George VI, he was inspired by the king's own triumph over the humiliation of stuttering. David's own cure involved learning to swear, and then asking a girl out on a date! Later as he matured into a writer, he felt an obligation to his royal hero and wanted to write a screenplay that brought to life the little-known details of Albert's life. After years of drafts and delays, it finally made it to the screen as *The King's Speech*. The heroic inspiration that David felt as a boy was now the experience of millions of viewers. Little wonder that it won the Oscar for the Best Picture in 2010.

Like Michael Landon and King George VI, when a man chooses to turn and face his shame, something irrevocable shifts inside. He quits running. He quits hiding. He refuses to cower and chooses to stand.

He becomes heroic.

THE POWER OF SHAME

Shame is a cruel tyrant with an immense dominion. No one escapes its sway. No one dodges its assault. At the same time, shame is also the unmentionable subject. Who speaks about it at dinner parties? What conversation among good friends broaches it? To speak about shame only evokes more shame. This one-two punch gives shame its silent, lockdown power.

What exactly is shame? It is the feeling of exposure before others that elicits their contempt. Our private flaws are broadcast for public display, and we feel branded and exiled. The sting of shame is so sharp that our response is immediate: we run for cover. The cover then becomes a way of maneuvering through life. This is the genesis of the false self.

During my sophomore year in high school, a friend invited me to attend a high school sorority presentation. He was dating a girl being presented, and she had a friend that needed an escort. I reluctantly agreed to the blind date. In keeping with the attire for the affair, I rented a tux, my first time in such formal clothing. But I had not anticipated the difficulties in putting it on. I turned the cummerbund inside and out, trying to figure out how to attach it around my waist, and my fingers fumbled putting on the cuff links. The real snag came when I couldn't find the bow tie. I assumed it was part of the outfit, but after searching through the rental packaging, no bow tie was found. I concluded that it must be optional.

Upon reaching the presentation, I realized that I was the only one without a bow tie. I immediately felt uneasy. That uneasiness turned to dread as I stood in the line to be presented. In a few minutes, I would step onto the stage with my date, and the spotlight would hit us, exposing me to all eyes. The dread turned into panic as I neared the stage. I wanted a hole to open in the floor, so I could drop down and disappear. Instead, I stepped up to meet my date with the glare of the spotlight blinding us. As I escorted her down the steps of the runway, I heard mocking comments from upperclassmen about my attire. I was horrified. The shame bit so deep that I didn't care about my date anymore. I just wanted to leave. When I did make it back home, I undressed and hung up the clothing to return to the tux store. Up in the top compartment of the hanger, I noticed a small box I had missed before. Inside was the bow tie. I now felt more shame and self-contempt for being such an idiot.

Along with other shaming experiences during those adolescent years, I contracted a way of positioning myself before others. I would never be caught unprepared again. Anything that involved an audience, I would meticulously plan out. I would not be exposed again. It was scripted down to the punctuation marks. The result? It brought me applause and affirmation. But it was a lie.

It was a false self.

One day in a conversation with Heidi, she commented that everything in my life felt scripted, even our relationship. The thought of being spontaneous or playful was impossible in my emotional vocabulary. She was right. I was an engineered, cardboard cutout. I looked good, but it was all a sham. I had been successful in avoiding more public humiliation, but in doing so, I had buried my true self.

THE TRAGEDY OF THE FALSE SELF

Everything that is real has the sharp edge of its reality rooted in God. The swaying trees, the mottled rocks, the sky-blue atmosphere, the salted sea—all creation is real because it has its being in God. Only God is the truly Real, and He has eagerly shared His realness in the created order. But when it comes to that part of the order created in His image, there is a distinct shift. We are given the privilege of participating in His reality. We are given a choice. We can choose the real or turn away.

Here lies the tragedy of shame. Covering ourselves doesn't feel like a choice but an escape from certain annihilation. It is a choice nonetheless. We choose to concoct what is not real, what can never be real, because it has no roots in God. It is a sham from start to finish. The tragedy is compounded because our false self then gets bound up in the chase for false glory. We are forever chasing after anything to keep the appearance of being strong and successful in the world's eyes. We are frauds running after frauds.

None of this has any sustainable reality because none of it is tied to God's being. The transient nature of our self-constructed heroic stories becomes apparent at some point. The invincible athlete gets injured and has to quit the sport. The unstoppable entrepreneur makes an arrogant decision and shipwrecks the company. The man with the showpiece wife discovers she has turned on him in an affair. Whatever the false self has relied on will collapse.

But the real tragedy of the false self lies with the heroic longing. The false man can never be the noble man. He can never be heroic. That false man is forever running and hiding. He is chained to a scheme of life that makes him a sucking vortex, pulling family, friends, and colleagues into its churning whirlpool, rending and drowning them. Shame is the culprit, making us acutely narcissistic. We are driven by the fear that we will be shamed again, so our emotional antennas have difficulty picking up any signal but our own. We cannot feel the weight of the souls around us. Everything rotates around our egocentric universe.

When Jesus calls a man to follow Him and die, His voice reaches into that false self. It must go. It must die.

It must be unmasked.

DISCOVERING THE TRUE SELF

Saying that is one thing. Attempting it is another. As with our disordered attachments, we are being asked to go where we have never been, to become what we do not know. How can you find a path through this uncharted territory where there seems to be no map and no guide? How do you discover your true self if it has been buried longer than you can remember?

The New Testament can offer some helpful direction. Paul exhorts us to put off the old self and put on the new (Eph. 4:22–24). The old self was chained to a way of being that has been dealt a deathblow by the cross of Christ. Yes, it can still be our default mode, but it's not real. It's an illusion. It has power over us only to the extent that we allow it. It can be thwarted. To put on the new self is to discover the true self, who we are in God's eyes. It is to let His love deal another deathblow, this time to shame. As we live in the gaze of that persistent love, our true self will begin to come out of hiding.

John encourages us along in this way: "But if we walk in the light, as he is in the light, we have fellowship with one another, and the blood of Jesus, his Son, purifies us from all sin" (1 John 1:7). To walk in the light is both unnerving and liberating. It is to walk in the light of God, who is Light Himself. God knows no shame, no hiding, no false self. He wears no mask. He is who He is. It is His piercing reality that calls us out of our falseness.

To walk in the light is also to remove our false selves before others. We tell our stories and confess our sins with those whom we trust. We unmask because walking in the light requires that. Recently, the community group I lead in our church spent an evening doing just that. Sins of jealousy, bitterness, and judgmentalism were confessed, as well as the lust for success and fame. In the unmasking, love was offered to all. We were learning to walk in the light.

Here is the second truly heroic thing a man now does. Along with letting go of his attachments, he faces his shame. He tells his story. He admits his sin and his idols. I have watched men do this on countless occasions. The response is universal. When a man unmasks before other men, there is respect and admiration. He has displayed courage. He has stared down the tyrant of shame and refused to cower. He is becoming heroic.

The irony is striking but goes even much deeper. When describing our chase for false glory, I mentioned Jeremiah's call to stop boasting in our strength and wisdom. Instead, we are to boast in the Lord, in His reality of love, kindness, and justice. How this is possible becomes clearer in the New Testament. Paul alludes to Jeremiah's command in a starting pronouncement: ". . . Christ the power of God and the wisdom of God. For the foolishness of God is wiser than man's wisdom and the weakness of God is stronger than man's strength" (1 Cor. 1:24–25). Jesus appeared to be weak and foolish, suffering the humiliation of the cross. There was no display of power or skill, might or wisdom. Instead, there was torture, disgrace, defeat, and finally death. But the cross is precisely how God breaks the spell of the false self. This is the strength that thrusts a sword into the heart of evil. This is the wisdom that breaks the spell of shame.

When a man chooses to come out of hiding and walk in the light, when he tells his story with forthrightness and candor, he is following in the way of the Great Hero. He is choosing what appears to be weak and foolish. Men are fixated on putting the game face on, impressing the competition, and scrambling to the top of the heap.

Who wants to appear weak and foolish before other men? Yet right here is the strength. Right here is the wisdom. Right here is the heroic.

THE POWER OF TRANSPARENCY

Let's turn it around the other way now. What would your life be like if you had no secrets and no shame? What would it feel like to live each day out of your true self as a man? We can only imagine such an enticing prospect. Yet there is One who lived this way. This was the secret of Jesus' remarkable life. He lived and breathed the glory of being the beloved Son of the Father. He had nothing to hide. He had no secrets to cover. During a heated debate with the Pharisees, he threw out an extraordinary challenge: "Can any of you prove me guilty of sin?" (John 8:46). Can you imagine saying such a thing? Can you imagine saying it before enemies who are greedily picking at anything you say to find some way to accuse you? Yet here is the power of transparency. He spoke the truth. He lived the truth. He was the truth. He had no false self.

It is this transparency that gave Him such astonishing courage before His enemies. His whole being was bent on setting the captive free, not on protecting Himself. He knew no shame, so His emotional energy was laser-focused on lifting others up. We can only gaze at such a life in awe. Yet we are to partake of such a life as men. Remember the whole point of His coming is to make us like Himself. He is the vanguard of the new creation. He is the pioneer of the new man.

What happens as we become transparent men? We give permission to other men to be transparent. I saw this displayed recently in one of my classes. During that time, I interviewed a friend who told his story of chasing false glory in his career and the unraveling of his life when one of his children fell into substance abuse. He shared the darkness of his soul and the light of Christ now saving him. After the interview, we broke up into small groups for discussion. One young man eagerly told of his own obsession with career, constantly comparing himself with other men in the process. He was so thankful for the interview and the hope it gave. He had been in the company of the weak and felt the strength.

THE WOUND BEHIND THE SHAME

The false self we construct is opposed to the new self in Christ. We must do what we can to unmask it. But in the end, this is beyond us. It is Jesus who must deconstruct it.

In that deconstruction, layers of shame and self-protection will need to be removed. There will be moments when we don't think we can keep going. There will be times of wilderness wandering. But there will also be stunning revelations along the way, encouraging us to keep going. The reason for our winding path is that Jesus is taking us behind the shame. He is taking us behind the self-protection. He is taking us into the wound.

Each man has some core wound that becomes the meter and measure of his soul. The wound may come from a father or family member. It may come from a teacher or coach. It may come from a peer or classmate. However it comes, the enemy of our souls then finds a way to keep pricking the wound, causing it to ooze and bleed again. Our response to this makes what is heart-breaking now tragic. We isolate and lick our wounds in private, thinking that this is the only way to find relief. But there is no healing here, only increasing infection and disease. But if we are willing, the Healer of our souls will move into this carefully guarded space and speak into the wound. How He does this for each man will be different. There is no formula, for each man's wound is unique.

The healing of my own wound came after years of peeling away the masks. I had made progress, but still felt bound by something I could not identify. My core wound still lay hidden in a memory fogged over by time. It was Jesus who pulled it up into my consciousness.

One morning as I was sitting in the silence in prayer, He brought it to mind. I was around thirteen and waking up to painful realities as a young man. I was in my father's bathroom alone staring at myself in the mirror. As I mulled over my standing with my peers at school, I was stung by shame. I hated myself and longed to be someone else more popular, more confident, more athletic. Yet that longing ricocheted back as despair. I could never be anyone else. I would always be stuck as me. I then walked out of my father's bathroom, using the right-hand door to my parents' bedroom. Hopelessness gripped me. This one memory was the core wound that had driven so much of my life. I could never feel at home inside of myself as a man. I was always grasping to be another man, despairing over myself. But as the memory surfaced, something unexpected happened.

As I imagined myself before the mirror again, Jesus was there in the bathroom. He didn't say anything or do anything. He just stood there looking at the reflection of me in the mirror. Then He opened the other door out of the bathroom, the left-hand door that went into my brother's room. But when he opened the door, I saw no bedroom, but a sweeping landscape of forest below me out of which mountain peaks arose in the distance. I knew there would be a descent to the forest floor and then mountains to climb. Jesus was telling me through these images that I would no longer be the man who always wanted to be someone else. I would come into my true self by following Him down into the forest and ascending the outlying peaks. It would be an arduous journey, but He would lead the way. All of this I knew with hearing a word from Him. In that moment, I knew that He knew my core wound. I knew He was going to heal me.

The time since that remarkable moment has been one of expanding freedom. I have traversed the dense forests and climbed the distant mountains. I see and feel things so differently now. I am becoming my own man, the one He had in mind. He is healing me. Helping other men along on the same journey has only added to the wonder. I am watching them become their own true selves. They, too, are following the great Healer and walking in the company of the unmasked.

It is the brotherhood of the heroic.

CHAPTER 10

THE FIGHT FOR IDENTITY

"In the social jungle of human existence, there is no feeling of being alive without a sense of identity."
—Erik Erikson, *Crisis of Identity*

"We have all read in scientific books, and, indeed, in all romances, the story of the man who has forgotten his name. This man walks about the streets and can see and appreciate everything; only he cannot remember who he is. Well, every man is that man in the story. Every man has forgotten who he is."
—G. K. Chesterton, *Orthodoxy*

I will also give that person a white stone with a new name written on it, known only to the one who receives it.
—Revelation 2:17

One of my unfortunate skills in life seems to be losing things of importance.

During my first year of marriage, I took a group of students tubing down a river on a hot summer day. Because of a dam upstream, any water released was frigid, having come from the bottom of the lake behind it. It was this ice-cold river that refreshed us in the sweltering heat. Toward the end of our ride, I was startled to find that my wedding band was gone. The cold had shrunk my fingers enough to allow it to fall off.

I once left my wallet on top of the car while opening the door to get in. As I turned out into traffic, the wallet flew off onto the shoulder of the road. The next day, I could not recall what I had done with it and felt sick about it. Then I got a call from the local donut shop. Someone had picked up the wallet on the road and had turned it in there. The credit cards were all there when I retrieved it, but the cash was gone.

But my stories (and there are many of them) do not compare with what happened to my sister. During our childhood, my family once visited a mining site long ago shut down as a commercial venture. Yet it still had small quantities of precious and semiprecious stones left in the soil. You could buy a bucket of dirt for a small fee and sift it, using a metal sieve and a chute of running water. I sat by that chute, with sieve in hand, examining scoop after scoop of dirt for what seemed like hours. I was rewarded for my patience with four small rubies.

My sister found her treasure another way. Climbing up onto the massive pile of dirt from which we took our bucketfuls, she suddenly spied something shiny lying on top of it. It turned out to be a huge garnet stone of ten carats! The stone was cut and then set in a necklace that she proudly wore. One day while playing in the woods in our backyard, it fell off, presumably from the clasp breaking. All attempts to find the necklace were in vain. She was heartbroken.

Some twenty-five years later, my father was cleaning out groundcover at the edge of the woods in the same backyard. Just like my sister, his eye caught something shiny lying on top of the ground. It was the lost necklace that everyone had long ago forgotten. Suddenly, to the delight of my sister, there it was! What had seemed lost forever was suddenly found.

I can think of no better analogy to what lies ahead on the heroic journey. Every man has lost something far more valuable than rings or wallets or garnet stones. This lost treasure has long ago passed out of conscious memory, and he is now used to surviving without it. But now, as he follows Jesus in the work of detaching and unmasking, something startling happens. What seemed lost forever is suddenly found. A man discovers who he really is. He finds his identity.

However startling the discovery, it is something the heroic tales have been telling us all along. Frodo thinks he is just a regular hobbit who would live out his days peaceably in the Shire. But he is the Ringbearer, the one who would save Middle Earth from Sauron's grip. In the Matrix myth, Mr. Anderson thinks he is just a cog in the corporate world. But he is more. He is Neo, the one who could conquer the Matrix and free the human race. Remember that identity is one of the two thematic poles around which all stories are constructed. The main character goes on a journey to accomplish something, and along the way, he finds out who he really is. This self-revelation is so critical that it often resolves the tension in the plot and brings the story to a happy end.

LOST IN NO-MAN'S LAND

As we move from story to reality though, there is a glaring disconnection. I see men everywhere who don't know who they are. Their outward folly and inward confusion are symptomatic of what is really going on. They are wandering in a no-man's land of lost identity.

My own story of lost identity traipses through large tracts of time. Some of it I have already told in the recurrent chase after fame, the stream of unhealthy attachments, and the shaming events that stole my heart. In my search for identity, I kept trying on different roles, much like a man would don different overcoats. I assumed that if I found the right one and wore it long enough, it would answer the question. But as I wandered through seasons as a songwriter, youth minister, church planter, Bible teacher, and running coach, it always felt as if I were plastering something on top, not living out of something blazing underneath. I believe this is the story of every man. We find something that seems to make us feel strong, something that wins the respect of men and the love of a woman, and cobble together some sense of who we are from it. This is our fallen identity. The price tag for such a maneuver is huge: our identity is forever chained to that role. When it changes, as it inevitably will, we are thrown back into the same no-man's land to wander again. But the biggest mistake behind our maneuver is the belief that identity can be self-constructed. Somehow we think we can figure out who we are.

To add to our wandering, so many toxic statements about our identity are deeply lodged in our hearts. They come from words hurled at us, or from words we have hurled at ourselves in shame: *I am such a loser. I will never be a man. I will never do anything good with my life. I am always the one left out. I am so stupid. I am unworthy of being loved. I am a weakling. I am on my own—no one will come for me. I am a nobody.* The list goes on and on, reinforced by events that only seem to prove the point. The one who believes he is a loser gets fired from his job. The one who believes he is stupid says something uninformed that invites scorn. The one who feels unworthy of being loved never finds someone to marry. The one who feels weak avoids anything requiring courage. The one who believes he is on his own keeps surface friendships. These identity statements rarely surface in day-to-day thoughts. Instead, they are locked away in distant memories that stain the way we feel about ourselves as men. When we come to faith in Jesus, we may hear the truth about our new identity as sons of the Father. We may understand that we are brothers of the living Christ. But the truth skips over the surface of our consciousness. It doesn't sink in.

Added confusion comes from a more sinister corner. And now we come to the real villain in our story. It's not those who block our way forward. It's not those who have wounded us. It's not even the things we have attached to for some sense of life. The real villain is Satan and his demonic hordes. And at the core level of identity, he does some of his best work. He is forever accusing, and the most virulent way to do that is to attack our identity. He is forever inciting us to find our identity in our work and then mocking us for our failure. Then he keeps jabbing us with those toxic lies, pinning us down in despair. In such a state, a man not only wanders in that no-man's land, but he wanders around hamstrung, forever limping and falling. It's impossible to plot any course toward the heroic life. He can barely walk.

So how does a man find out who he is? How does he solve the riddle of his identity? The answer is simple. He can't. Our lost identities can never be found by looking for them. The riddle will never be solved by more searching. There is only One who knows who we are. There is only One who knows our true identity. And He has to reveal it to us.

But we will have to fight to keep it.

THE FIGHT BEGINS

No man regains his true sense of self by wishful thinking in a few moments of clarity. The stakes are way too high. The battleground is way too contested. But the Scriptures give us some ammo in the fight. Listen to these declarations of New Testament truth: *I am a beloved son of God. I am forgiven and washed clean. I can never be condemned in Christ. I can never be separated from His love. I have the righteousness of Christ. I have every spiritual blessing in Christ. I am an heir with Christ. I am no longer a slave to fear. I have authority over the demonic. I have the Holy Spirit dwelling inside. I am the salt of the earth. I am the light of the world.* The list goes on and on, reinforced by the power of the resurrected Christ. As we let these truths wash over us, Jesus will coach us as to how to own them for ourselves. But it will be a fight to stay there. Here's why.

The lies that have formed our fallen identity will not be easily whisked away. It will be hand-to-hand combat, going into each door of the heart, flushing out the lie residing there, replacing it with the truth, and guarding that door from further assault. That assault will come at us from multiple angles. The world will keep insisting that our identity is wrapped up in career success, luring us with its tinsel glory. The false self will haunt us at times, urging us to run and hide again behind one of our well-used facades. The devil will also do his part. He will impale us with guilt that our identity is nothing but the sin we keep committing. He will pierce us with shame that our identity is no more than the wounds we have received. We then hear his diabolical whisper in the gloom of the night: *There's no use trying to change. You never will. You might as well give up. This is all you are.*

CALLING FORTH THE WARRIOR

This is when the fight gets ugly. Some days the battle is relentless. Other days it tracks us quietly in the background, only to break out in an unexpected skirmish. We get fatigued on the battle line. We get disoriented in the barrage. Resistance feels futile. Surrender feels inevitable. Yet here on this battleground, we are being taught to fight and stand. It's the training ground for the heroic life. The warrior in us is being called forth, and

Jesus is doing the calling. He will be our faithful commander in the fray. Here are some battle stories.

One of my friends grew up in a home where his mother tragically died when he was a boy. The father who remained was bitter and physically abusive. To add to the struggle, he recently faced off with cancer in his body and crises in his family. There are many times when it would have been easier for him to surrender. He has chosen not to. He has chosen to fight. One day he showed me an exhaustive list of identity statements from the New Testament printed out on a sheet of paper front and back. He keeps that paper close by and will often start his day repeating them to himself, declaring them to be true for him no matter what is going on around him. These declarations pierce the darkness. It's his way to fight.

Another friend of mine pastors a small church. He is barraged at times with the feeling that he is a second-class minister in a second-class church. He becomes envious of pastors with large churches and is then tempted to get others to like him so they will join his church. The pulls become relentless to seek the approval of others and live in fear of what they think. His only way out of the jungle is to enter the silence with God each morning and remember who he is. He is a beloved son. He is not second-class. He is not a slave to fear. It's his way of being a warrior, looking to Jesus in the fray. But even in the fight, sometimes the Lord Himself will have to rescue us.

The men's ministry I lead was sponsoring an open house that was part fund-raiser, part fellowship. Along with roasting a whole pig, there was a shooting range, football games on TV, and a fire pit. As folks dropped in from lunch through the dinner hour, everyone seemed to be having a good time. Everyone except me. I kept circling back in my thoughts to all those who had been invited who weren't there. One of my triggers for shame is to ask others to come to something and have only a few show up. The public exposure as a perceived failure then overwhelms me. This is exactly what happened. While cleaning up after the event, the shame that had gnawed at me flooded in. The evil one then drenched me in lies: *You are not cut out for this. You never were. You are nothing but a failure. It's time to give this ministry up. It will never go anywhere.* It was the mental equivalent of being punched in the stomach repeatedly. By the time I was driving home, I was writing a resignation letter to the board in my head. I couldn't fight anymore.

But it was all a lie. The event had opened the doors for so many reconnections among old friends. It was also wildly successful as a fund-raiser. I did not know that then. So Jesus had to come and rescue me the next morning. I had been asked to help in the Sunday service by leading the congregation in prayer. Still reeling from the previous evening, I spoke as best I could the truth of the Father's love out loud in that prayer. Without any faith on my part, it unexpectedly ambushed the darkness and sent the lies fleeing. I was not a failure. I was a beloved son of God. I walked up to pray a defeated man; I walked down ready to fight on.

THE RENAMING BEGINS

But more ammunition is needed in the fight for our identities. The battle is that intense. The war is that consuming. The truths from Scripture about our new identity in Christ are compelling, but they are generic. A man needs more. He longs for more. Is he just a nameless drop in the sea of humanity, or does he have a special place in the heart of God? Does God really notice him? Does God really see him?

It is here we find God revealing the mystery of a man's identity. He reveals it in a new name, a name that shows how God feels about him. It is such a stark contrast to the names most men give themselves: *My name is Stupid. My name is Vile. My name is Sinner. My name is Worthless. My name is Addict. My name is Reprobate. My name is Nobody.* It is heartbreaking to hear it stated this way, but that's exactly how they feel about themselves. They need healing. They need renaming.

We also need a new name because our given names are not enough. Our parents named us for someone admired in the family, for some trait they hoped would be ours, or simply because they liked the name. As a parent myself, I know our intentions are well-meaning with such names, but we do not know the secret of our children's souls. Their names do not call out their true identities. My name is a case in point. My parents named me William because they liked the name. It comes from the German word for *helmet* and is a metaphor for strength. When I first discovered this, I was impressed. But the revelation didn't translate beyond that. It didn't make me feel any stronger as a man. It didn't give me the courage to push through or the energy to endure. It was just the name I was called.

The name God has for us is different. It's what He created us to be and how He sees us. It's the secret of our souls. The renaming begins in the Old Testament with the idol-worshipper Abram. God calls him out and renames him Abraham, the one who would be the father of many nations. In the New Testament, Jesus renames faltering Simon as Peter, the rock of the church. Each of these men was situated at a turning point in the history of redemption. Each needed to know that he was so much more than who he thought he was.

No better story of renaming can be found in the Bible than the story of Jacob (Gen. 32:22–32). Jacob means "one who grasps the heel." Being a twin, he was delivered holding on to the heel of his brother, Esau. But the name means more than a birthing anomaly. Grasping the heel was an idiomatic way of describing deception, much the same way as we speak of someone pulling our leg. Jacob lived up to that name, manipulating and deceiving to get his way, starting with buying his brother's birthright as the first-born son for some lentil stew. It then escalated into disguising himself as Esau to steal the blessing from their blind father, Isaac. But being a deceiver was not who Jacob really was. God saw something so much more.

In the great crisis of his life, we find him running from Esau, fearing retribution and death at his brother's hands. Alone in the night, he is assaulted by an unknown wrestler who jumps out of the darkness.

Although this wrestler seemed unable to win the fight, he suddenly dislocates Jacob's hip. Somehow Jacob realizes this is no mere man, but somehow God Himself. He asks for the blessing, not by manipulation or deception but now by pleading: "I will not let you go unless you bless me." God responds with an unexpected question: "What is your name?" God is not after information. He is setting Jacob up for a monumental shift. After Jacob states his name, God delivers the announcement: "Your name will no longer be Jacob, but Israel, because you have struggled with God and with [men] and have overcome." God saw something else besides a deceiver. He saw an overcomer. His new name Israel revealed the passion of a man who struggled all his life to obtain the blessing by his own efforts. Now that passion was to be channeled into prayer. And that prayer would be heard and answered. Jacob received the ultimate blessing, the blessing of a new name. But he walked away from that night of wrestling with a limp. It, too, was a blessing, a disruptive one that would be a continual reminder of his new name. It was so significant that it became the name of God's Old Testament people.

A watershed is crossed when a man receives a new name. He begins to feel what God feels toward him and finds the authority to reject all the fallen identities. Hints of this watershed crossing happen whenever we are recast in the eyes of another. Recently, I was able to reconnect with one of my high school teachers. He has long since retired, but had vivid memories of me. I prodded him for stories about former teachers and students, and he responded with story after story. Eventually, I came around to the question hanging in my soul. I had so many painful memories of high school, and I longed to know something else. So I mustered the courage to ask: *How did you see me then?* I think he was surprised at the question, but quickly answered with the school motto: "Bill, I always saw you as a gentleman, scholar, and athlete." It was the answer I never expected. It caught me off guard. The terrible images I had of myself during that time melted. That's how he saw me. Perhaps that's who I was. Remember, a man's identity can never be self-constructed. It must come from another.

When we move from how another man sees us to how God does, the mystery deepens. So does the trans-formation. How He sees us is who we truly are. The Creator knows His creation like no one else. But how do we find our true name? We do just what I did with my high school teacher. We ask and stay open for the answer. There is no formula for how our names will come to us. I can't give you a set of steps to follow. God will approach each of us in the way we need. It may come as a word spoken or as an image offered. It may come as an actual name or as a phrase to consider. It may come through the reading of Scripture or the reading of a heroic story. And it will often come when we least expect it.

But if we ask, we will receive.

My first experience of being renamed came on a backpacking trip I took with some men. I was hiking on my own at one point, with my friends ahead or behind. I remember walking beside a small stream on the left with bamboo stalks rising high on the right. The path was clearly cut, so I was not thinking about the hike. I wasn't thinking about anything important, and I don't even remember praying. What I do remember is an unexpected whisper in my soul: "You are My treasure." I couldn't believe what I was hearing, so I responded in doubt, "What?" Again, there was the gentle whisper: "You are My treasure." There was no mistake about whose voice it was. But it was difficult to receive. My inward response was typical for that time: "Okay, that was strange."

Here's the backstory. So much of my inner life had been constructed around feeling unworthy of love. The only love I could find was through achieving success in some endeavor and receiving the applause of onlookers. I received admiration for what I did, but not love for who I was. I could perform well, but in the secret places of my heart, I felt shame and aloneness. Into those secret places, God was delivering that word: "You are My treasure."

That night around the campfire, we all processed the events of the day. With some hesitancy, I told my story. Would my friends think I was weird? I even doubted myself. Was I just hearing my own thoughts? I had to find out. When I came home from the backpacking trip, I looked up the word *treasure* in a Bible concordance. It took me to Exodus 19:5: "Now if you obey me fully and keep my covenant, then out of all nations you will be my treasured possession." My stomach flipped. The words spoken to God's people then were spoken to me now. This is how God saw me. I was His treasure. I was the Treasured One. This was my name before Him.

Countless times I have held onto that name in the chaos of the battle. It anchors me like few things.

My experience is not unique but paralleled by other brothers I know. My friend who watched *Star Wars* over and over as a young man also found his new name. The character of Luke Skywalker deeply resonated with him at that age because he felt so abandoned by his father and other men. He longed for an older man to come and mentor him, as Obi-Wan did for Luke. As he grew in the faith, he sensed that God's new name for him was Luke. But one day while praying, this is what he heard from the Lord: "No, you are *my* Luke." To be God's Luke meant that God was personally coming for him. It spoke into his fatherless soul, affirming the longing and healing the wound. He is a man growing into his new name.

What happens when a man is renamed? He learns to own who he is before God and no longer caters to the expectations of others. He is becoming his own man. He is becoming heroic. That core sense of identity becomes a deep well of strength from which he can draw as he follows Jesus into the heroic journey. And he will need every drop of that strength for what lies ahead. Every hero is not only given an identity to own but a quest to take. To that part of the heroic journey, we now turn.

CHAPTER 11

THE SHAKING
OF THIS WORLD

*"For the Quest is achieved, and now all
is over. I am glad you are here with me.
Here at the end of all things, Sam."*
—J. R. R. Tolkien, *The Lord of the Rings*

*"I have found that there are three stages in
every great work of God: first, it is impossible,
then it is difficult, then it is done."*
—Hudson Taylor

*"Very truly I tell you, whoever believes in
me will do the works I have been doing,
and they will do even greater things than
these, because I am going to the Father."*
—John 14:12

Lincoln is always at or near the top of polls concerning America's best president. Not being a historian, I had always admired him from afar. That admiration was brought much closer when I went to see the movie *Lincoln*. The film let me experience his high-pitched voice, his folksy drawl, and his homespun humor. I watched him play with his youngest son, lead an unruly cabinet, struggle with his grieving wife, and treat aides with a human touch. Of course, the end of the story is no surprise. What surprised me, though, was my response. Having died from the assassination bullet, Lincoln lay lifeless in his bed surrounded by mourning friends and family. His one-time political enemy, now Secretary of War Edwin M. Stanton, then uttered those historic words: "Here lies the most perfect ruler of men the world has ever seen. Now he belongs to the ages." As he spoke that tribute, I broke into tears. My admiration for Lincoln had become love for him as a father figure. And now I had lost him. Grief shook me.

As I reflected on my tears, I realized that Lincoln's life mirrored so many of the heroic tales. Despite his flaws, he had a clear sense of what he was to do with his life. That clarity seemed to emanate from a recurrent dream: He was alone on some vast vessel moving at great speed through water toward an indefinite shore. Before each important event of the war, the dream occurred, and it always foreboded a favorable outcome. In the movie, his wife, Mary, gave the dream added color. She felt it had to do with his desire to get the 13th Amendment to abolish slavery through Congress. Lincoln clearly accepted the idea that God can speak to men through dreams as He did in the Bible. The dream seemed to reveal something about his quest. He was the one man, the only man, who could lead the nation through the chaos of the Civil War to a new place it had never been. Lincoln needed this reassurance to keep pressing toward reunion. It also fueled his passion to get the 13th Amendment through Congress. For him, slavery was an indefensible evil poisoning the country. It must be eliminated. And he was the one who could do it. Lincoln accepted his quest and got the amendment passed. But he paid for it with his life. I then realized that I loved Lincoln not only as a father figure but as a hero. His life shook the world.

Lincoln's story can be repeated in so many of the great heroes of the faith: Paul and Peter, Chrysostom and Augustine, St. Patrick and St. Francis, Luther and Wesley, Bonhoeffer and Lewis. Although their stories are unique, they were all men who shook the world. Their sense of mission propelled them forward no matter what the obstacles were, no matter what the cost entailed. They left the mark of a hero. What man doesn't want to leave such a mark? What man doesn't want to shake the world? But how does he get there? How does it happen?

It happens when Jesus marks him.

MARKED WITH A QUEST

Let's go back again to the heroic journey in literature. The quest is the central motif around which all stories are constructed. The hero is given a task to do, a mission to accomplish. It becomes the driving energy around which everything in the plot happens. Frodo has to find a way into Mordor and destroy the ring. Luke Skywalker must take on the Dark Side of the Force and defeat it. Maximus must revenge the death of his family and restore justice to Rome. The structure of the great stories is shouting something to every man. Art is reflecting life. To become a man, you must be propelled by a mission. To become heroic, you must be fueled by a quest.

That shout resonates inside of men, and the resonance ignites a raging fire. It's what drove underage American boys to lie about their age so that they could enlist in World War II. It's what propelled men to enter the rigors of the Apollo astronaut program with the goal of landing a man on the moon. It's what drove Edmund Hillary and Tenzing Norgay to summit Mount Everest for the first time in 1953, despite the massive risks from frostbite, altitude sickness, and ice crevasses. It's what kept Lewis and Clark traversing endless mountain ranges in their mission to find a route across America to the Pacific. So many of the underdog sports stories tell the same tale. Recently, I read *The Boys in the Boat*, chronicling the quest of nine college rowers from the University of Washington, who set out to do the impossible—win Olympic gold. Despite the unimaginable obstacles they faced, they not only succeeded, but did so in Hitler's Germany in 1936. The story reads like one of the great heroic myths, except this one really happened.

The fiery longing for a quest is perhaps the truest thing we know about ourselves as men. To take up the quest is to focus the soul with purpose. It is to fill the heart with passion for the seemingly impossible. And to do this with other men forges a brotherhood never found elsewhere. We instinctively know that answering the call of the quest is our best hope of becoming a man. Yet it is also the most confusing. How are we to answer that call without once again constructing our own heroic stories, chasing after fame, power, and success? We already know the end of those journeys—disaster and defeat.

The answer lies with the Great Hero. As we follow His coaching, He will ask us to detach from our idols and unmask the old self. This is our initiation into the heroic life through death. But all of this is preparatory. We are to die so that we can awaken as men with a new identity. And as we awaken, Jesus will mark each of us with a quest. It is this mark that sets us ablaze. It is this mark that shakes the world.

But first we have some backtracking to do.

RECEIVING A QUEST

When Jesus called His men, He gave them a new identity as His disciples, but He also gave them something to do. All of that time spent with Him was a training ground for their mission. After His resurrection, they were now to advance the Kingdom He had inaugurated. His quest was to be theirs, one that would consume the rest of their lives: "Therefore go and make disciples of all nations, baptizing them in the name of the Father and of the Son and of the Holy Spirit, and teaching them to obey everything I have commanded you" (Matt. 28:19–20). That same quest is given to all who follow the Master. But that only raises more questions: How does a man discover his unique part in this mission? How does he gain clarity about his role in advancing the Kingdom?

The answer is surprisingly similar to finding one's identity. The quest is not something you find. It finds you.

There is no formula for what happens next. How God will reveal to each man his mission can never be scripted. We see this over and over in the biblical narrative. God called Jeremiah to be a prophet during his teen years, but He called Moses out of the desert at eighty. Joseph got a hint of his quest in a dream before his brothers threw him into a pit. Samuel received his mission when God called his name out in the night. Isaiah got his assignment in a vision where he saw the God of holiness on His throne. Others like Gideon got a sudden angelic visitation. Still others, like Nehemiah, discerned their mission as just an unshakable burden of what they had to do. For Peter, it came in a new name that was both an identity and a quest: he was to be the rock of the newly formed church.

To make matters more uncertain, the quest each man is given is different. What he is asked to do takes into account his own unique background, gifts, and temperament. There is no pattern except that God initiates the quest. And that quest can change as the years go by. This was certainly the case for me. My call into the ministry in my early twenties came through a tap on my shoulder from a pastor. It was the furthest thing from my mind at that point. My mission of teaching Bible to high school students in my mid-thirties came through an unexpected phone call. I was at first resistant and initially turned down the offer. My present quest of working with men came through a bizarre series of conversations, events, and divine promptings. One pivotal moment happened this way:

I was driving my Ford pickup one fall day on a familiar route home that took me through a nearby park. I wasn't thinking about anything important, certainly not my mission. At the time, I was in the beginning stages of this new work with men. I had more questions than answers, more fear than faith. None of this was on my mind though. I was just gazing at the scenery, enjoying the view of a sun-soaked landscape that stretched out on both sides of the road. Unbidden, a quiet whisper came. It was so soft that I could barely hear it in the back reaches of my mind. I had to lean in to listen: "Your name is Healer." I immediately knew whose voice it was.

The name became a revelation about my whole life. Much of my college experience had been spent studying pre-medicine, only to find out that I hated being around sick people while interning with a doctor. So after dropping pre-med, I wandered through the rest of my college days disoriented about career. In addition, I identified so strongly with characters in stories who were healers. For example, Aragorn in *The Lord of the Rings* was a master healer, using his skill with herbs to heal the wounds of war. He lived up to the ancient prophecy: "The hands of the king are the hands of a healer."[11] Then there was the mystery of my own healing. My college years were disorienting for another reason: I became soul-sick from depression and demonic oppression. After years of struggling with both, God spoke clearly one day into my soul: "I want to heal you." Those five words became reality as He took me on a journey of personal healing. Now He was asking me to pay it forward. The name Healer was not so much an affirmation as it was a quest. It was my part to play. I was to be a healer of men. It didn't answer all the questions. But it was the point around which my heart became laser-focused.

But do not take my story as the way the quest will come to you. It may not come in the form of a name. It may come in a random email or in a vivid dream. It may come while conversing with a friend or while reading the Bible. It may come during a moment of quiet prayer or during the hubbub of work. God will come to each man as He chooses in a time and place that is right, often by surprise. This way, we know that the quest is not another one of our self-constructed schemes. It comes delivered to us, with our name on the envelope. We may open it or toss it in the trash, but we know we didn't write the letter.

Our part in all this is to ask and keep our hearts open. Remember, if you ask, you will receive. This is one of the rules of the Master's house. He does not play favorites. Trust me, He will find you.

THE PERILS OF THE QUEST

But by definition, a quest is not something easily taken or accomplished. We will become exposed to perils that will test us, expose us, and sometimes derail us. There will be moments when we want to give up or give in. My friend Carter calls it hiking above the tree line, where you are exposed to dramatic temperature changes, afternoon lightning, and howling winds.

Our hesitation is understandable. Life seems perilous enough as it is. Men get cancer and die. They suffer financial loss. They have children who go AWOL and spouses who walk away. They endure life-altering car accidents, deceitful business partners, and unjust firing from jobs. With such dangers all around, our response is understandable: hunker down, get rid of as much risk as possible, and protect yourself. We then try to construct a safe life for ourselves. It is this self-protective scheme that is upended by the quest. We are being asked to protect others and serve them instead. This is the mind-set of the heroic man. But unnumbered dangers will meet him as he goes.

The great myths have repeatedly told us of such perils. Every one of them contains apparent defeats, when it looks like it's all over for the hero. Frodo's quest to take the ring to Mordor became so difficult that if it weren't for Sam at his side, he would have given up. Maximus was nearly executed and had to face death repeatedly as a gladiator until he could face off with Commodus. William Wallace faced the ultimate peril of a hero: he was tortured and killed by the English.

The questions now come quickly: *What kind of perils will I face? What will I have to endure? Will I be able overcome?* These questions and many others surface when a man thinks about the dangers of a quest. But remember what was roused in the fight for identity: the warrior spirit. That fight was a training ground to prepare a man for this battle. It is this warrior who can face down the perils of a quest and not capitulate. What perils am I speaking of? There are many, but two seem universal.

The quest will inevitably take us into our deepest fear. There is something hidden in every man that gnaws at him: a crippling shame, a persistent sin, a defining failure. The fear it incites sends him running away, but that running doesn't make the fear go away. It defines him, making him feel branded as a coward. The call of the quest will ask a man to do what seems unthinkable—to quit running and turn into the fear. No wonder he shies away from the call. No wonder he refuses it at first. Moses made excuses about his voice. Gideon claimed to be too weak. Jeremiah balked because of his youth. To be obedient, they had to stop running. They had to face the fear.

In the peculiar providence of God, this is His way of healing a man both of the fear and the wound behind the fear. Instead of refusing the quest, he now refuses to listen to fear. The voice of fear will still murmur and hiss, but the warrior has been awakened. He has heard the call. He takes up shield and sword and starts thinking like a warrior. He puts his best skills to work and uses whatever cunning he has to get going. Once that warrior gets moving on his quest, anything can happen. This is how God makes us into men. This is how He molds us into heroes. This is how He shakes the world.

A number of years ago, I spoke at a retreat to men of all ages, including fathers and sons. It was my first time to address so large a gathering, and I felt the exhilaration of speaking into the masculine soul. After the last session, I went home exhausted and quickly fell into a deep sleep that afternoon. I awoke after an hour or so, but stayed in that foggy borderland between sleep and consciousness. There I saw myself standing with my feet covered by a churning fog, much like the dry ice effects you see on a stage. I knew without being told what it was. It was evil. It was the evil one himself. I had a sword with me and raised it up as high as I could with both hands over my head. As I plunged it down into the swirling cloud with all my might, I cursed evil and declared: "To stop me, you will have to kill me." I jolted awake. Was it a dream? Was it a vision? Whatever it was, I was stunned by the passion with which I had spoken. Despite my fears, God was rousing the warrior. I could never go back to what I once was. I didn't want to either. Whatever perils awaited me, I wanted to go down swinging away, not running away.

Along with our deepest fears, another universal peril of the quest involves its very nature. We love the idea of the quest as long as it's manageable and within our capacity. But the quest God gives us is never like that. It is not something we can pull off with a little more sweat equity. The task He gives us is so far beyond us. It is impossible from the start.

Every great work of the Kingdom started out as an impossibility. William Carey sat at his cobbler's bench in England, praying over the world, deeply concerned about the millions who had no chance to hear of Jesus. Despite ministerial criticism and unimaginable obstacles, he founded a mission in India and became the father of the modern-day missions movement.

William Wilberforce knew that God had called him to use his position to abolish slavery in England. In a forty-five-year battle with Parliament, he endured an onslaught of slander and countless defeats. But three days before he died, Parliament finally passed the Slavery Abolition Act.

Disenfranchised with Communism as a Russian soldier, Aleksandr Solzhenitsyn began to criticize the government and was sent to one of the infamous Soviet labor camps. During the suffering he endured there, he wrote novels exposing the lies of Communism and the truth of God. His works became one of the major catalysts for the downfall of the Soviet Union.

There are countless stories like these throughout church history. In each one, a man takes up the quest and ends up shaking the world. How did it happen? Jesus told us that the work of building His kingdom was not to come through our best efforts but through the power of God. Remember, it's His kingdom we are building, not ours. When we have taken on this way of thinking, we quit fixating on the obstacles and announcing retreat. We start asking God for a way through them. We are to become men that don't just climb mountains. We are to move them.

WHAT HAPPENS TO A MAN ON A QUEST

Whatever perils await a man on his quest, it is a watershed moment when he chooses to take it. Everything starts to tighten down and focus. You remember those amoebas from high school biology? They were the single-cell blobs of protoplasm roaming aimlessly and eating whatever they could find. There is no more fitting image for a man without a quest. He is an amoeba on two legs, without shape to his soul. He wanders aimlessly, seeking pleasure in everything and consuming it as he does.

With a quest, everything changes. A man moves from an amoeba to an arrow. Everything snaps to attention—his gifts, his experiences, his passions. He becomes lean and pointed. His reputation, his safety, even his success—all that becomes secondary or inconsequential. He is a man on the move with a target in sight. Life now becomes the wild adventure he could have never scripted for himself. He feels that wildness in his soul as he takes on the impossible in the name of Jesus.

Along with the wildness, the quest will tap into an underground source of strength he didn't know existed inside. That strength will become a massive flood bursting the dams of fear and shame that had bound him. As the dams crumble and wash away, he will experience the release of such a cleansing. It is the release of joy. It is the joy of finding out what God has written into our hearts from the very beginning. It is unrolling the scroll for our lives, the script that joins our deepest desires and with God's calling. What God hopes we will do in this life is inscribed in those deep desires. I say this to negate the ridiculous notion that the quest God gives us will make us miserable. The exact opposite is true. The foundation of the heroic life is joy, indomitable joy, and everything we say and do on the quest will move us along on that foundation.

The apostle Paul was the epitome of a man who lived in that joy. The resurrected Christ summoned him to take the message of the Kingdom to all the Gentiles. He took up that quest and shook the world. Listen to this man's arrow-like focus: "For to me, to live is Christ and to die is gain" (Phil. 1:21). Hear how he refused self-protection to serve others: "I ask you, therefore, not to be discouraged because of my sufferings for you, which are your glory" (Eph. 3:13). This is how he faced impossibilities at every turn: "Now to him who is able to do immeasurably more than all we ask or imagine, according to his power that is at work within us" (Eph. 3:20). Here is the warrior in him awakened: "No, in all these things we are more than conquerors through him who loved us" (Rom. 8:37). Listen to the litany of perils he endured as that warrior:

> Five times I received from the Jews the forty lashes minus one. Three times I was beaten with rods, once I was pelted with stones, three times I was shipwrecked, I spent a night and a day in the open sea, I have been constantly on the move. I have been in danger from rivers, in danger from bandits, in danger from my fellow Jews, in danger from Gentiles; in danger in the city, in danger in the country, in danger at sea; and in danger from false believers. I have labored and toiled and have often gone without sleep; I have known hunger and thirst and have often gone without food; I have been cold and naked. (2 Cor. 11:24–27)

Yet despite all of this, his foundation was invincible joy: "I am greatly encouraged; in all our troubles my joy knows no bounds" (2 Cor. 7:4). "Rejoice in the Lord always. I will say it again: Rejoice!" (Phil. 4:4). Finally, listen to this noble warrior as he faced death: "I have fought the good fight, I have finished the race, I have kept the faith" (2 Tim. 4:7). He had done it. The quest was achieved. And the world has never been the same.

Ignatius closed all of his letters the same way: "Go and set the world on fire." That's what Paul did. That's what the saints through the ages have done. That's what every man can do who takes up his quest.

CHAPTER 12

THE SECRET OF GREATNESS

*"No one who has come to true greatness
has not felt in some degree that his life
belongs to the people, and what God has
given them he gives it for mankind."*
—Phillips Brooks

*"In the Kingdom of God, service is not a
stepping-stone to nobility: it is nobility, the
only kind of nobility that is recognized."*
—T. W. Manson

*Who, being in very nature God, did not
consider equality with God something to be
used to his own advantage; rather, he made
himself nothing by taking the very nature of
a servant, being made in human likeness.*
—Philippians 2:6–7

You often hear it on the TV news—the story of a man
who has performed some heroic deed. It could be pulling
a child from a burning house, protecting a bystander
from a terrorist bullet, or plucking flood victims out of
a raging river. Often the rescuer will be asked, "What's
it like to be a hero?" The man's response is inevitably

along these lines: "I don't really feel like a hero. I just saw someone in need."

We don't give such a reply much thought, but if we probe a bit, that familiar response is confusing. If a man who has just risked his life to save someone doesn't feel heroic, then who would qualify? What man would ever make it there? Probing a bit deeper, it raises another question that has been lurking in the background throughout this exploration of the heroic: What does it feel like to be heroic? Yes, that's the question at hand. Is the heroic feeling what a warrior has when he looks over his conquest? Is it the feeling an athlete gets when he perseveres against all odds and receives the prize? Is it winning the admiration of an audience or the love of a woman or the respect of competitors? We may feel joy, triumph, or honor in such situations, but feeling heroic is not one of them. This is the great irony of the heroic man. He's not interested in finding some kind of heroic status before the eyes of others. He's not even thinking about being heroic.

He's too busy thinking about everyone else.

I know this firsthand from spending years with a man who was my former boss. He became the principal of the struggling high school where I taught and led it into a season of flourishing. The student morale shifted from sullen to energized. Shame about the school gave way to a pride in what was happening. This same type of turnaround happened in several other schools under his leadership. His secret wasn't updated educational norms or motivational speeches. It wasn't streamlining procedures or better discipline. It wasn't even visionary thinking. His secret was much simpler.

On many mornings you would find him standing by the main entrance to the school, greeting students as they entered. It was his way to connect to many of them with a smile and a word of encouragement. He would also move around to teachers in their classrooms, checking in to see if they needed anything. He hated sitting in his office, roaming the halls instead as he looked for ways to engage students. He made a special point to listen intently before ever judging a situation, even with an unruly student or a cranky parent. One of the most striking things about him was his method of discipline. He would have the difficult conversation with offenders and mete out appropriate consequences. But after time was served, he would find ways to reconnect with them, often taking them out fishing with him. There amongst the poles and tackle, the heart conversations would happen and the real restoration would begin. Teachers would come by his office just to talk with him, often about personal problems more than school issues. I was one of those who took that opportunity whenever I could.

Watching him in action was the best leadership training I have ever received. He never led from the top with fiat declarations. He always led from the middle, sensing the needs around him and influencing others from there. One of his favorite sayings was this: "Ministry is only an arm's length away." He taught me to see every interaction as a place for ministry, even when it was discipline.

What was his secret? It's simple. He served.

It's the secret of greatness. It's the secret of becoming heroic.

GREATNESS THROUGH SERVING

But such a conclusion is difficult to swallow. The word *heroic* is so hyper-loaded with images of grandeur and dazzle. The heroes we idolized as boys seemed to radiate an ethereal greatness. Then we try to grab at that greatness in our lust for false glory. Our thoughts spiral around the bigger, the higher, the greater. We think the answer is to climb. The heroic must be at the summit. But it is not true. There is no air and no life at the summit. There is no greatness either, only disappointment and agitation, and if a man stays there, a darkening of the eye and a crumbling of the soul. The men who have clawed their way to the top have been stumbling into an abyss all along. Here, the only prize is smallness of heart and puniness of soul.

I have always loved the sonnet by Percy Bysshe Shelley titled "Ozymandius." It tells of an ancient statue of a king, colossal in proportion, but now in complete ruins. Only its massive legs still stand with the shattered face lying on the drifting sand beside them. But the words on the pedestal can still be read: "My name is Ozymandias, King of Kings; Look on my Works, ye Mighty, and despair!" Around the remains of the statue, there is nothing but desert, stretching in all directions. This is the legacy of the man who claws his way to the summit.

Contrast this with a movie that has become a Christmas tradition. It ranks near the top of the American Film Institute's top one hundred movies, having received countless honors and awards. It has consistently grown in popularity over the last seventy years with no signs of waning. Both director Frank Capra and actor Jimmy Stewart said it was the favorite film of their careers. You may recognize the movie now: *It's a Wonderful Life.* The plot is so well known that it needs no retelling. What does need telling is this: George Bailey was a hero in every sense of the word. But he was not someone gifted with extraordinary pedigree or skill. He was not building some huge enterprise. He had no fame or national following. He just used his family bank to help his fellow townsfolk buy their own homes. Somehow in the ordinary business of serving others, he became extraordinary. In the end, all those he had helped came back to serve him, saving him from bankruptcy and ruin. George really had a wonderful life. He mattered to so many people. He found the secret of greatness.

The story of George Bailey carries such formidable sway. I have used this movie in my own teaching, only to find the audience in tears at the end of the clip. The film unearths that piercing hope we all have to matter and to be celebrated. This is the longing for glory. It was to be our continual inheritance from God and our heartbeat as men. But now the loss of that glory is so fraught with anguish that we frantically seek any means to attain it. So begins the tragic hunt for false glory. But George Bailey did it differently. Whatever dreams of grandeur he had as a young man he chose to let them go to help his struggling neighbors. Without even realizing what was happening, he became great in the eyes of everyone in Bedford Falls. He found glory. And he did it by serving.

THE WARRIOR AS SERVANT

But the word *serve* still falls on deaf ears for so many men. It does not conjure up masculine images of strength and glory, but ones of groveling before others, losing the power to choose, and even being used and abused. The images exude weakness and impotence. I can think of few demonic lies with more power. It's time to expose the lie.

The Samurai of Japan were known for their skill in fighting and heroism in battle. What's not so well known is the meaning of the word *samurai*. It is derived from a Japanese word meaning *to serve*. The Samurai warriors existed to serve the emperor and the empire and to give their lives if necessary in their defense.

This same ethos frames our own military. I will never forget my invitation along with other educators to visit the Marine Corps Boot Camp at Paris Island, South Carolina. It's a shrewd marketing device the Marines use, and it works. Teachers go back and sell the Marines to their students. I was certainly sold. There for a few days, we were allowed to experience the training firsthand. As we pulled up to the curb in a bus, a drill sergeant was unleashed on us, exploding onto the bus and yelling at us to get out and line up on the sidewalk.

It's the same thing that happens to new recruits. We got to fire the guns used in their training, peering through sights at targets hundreds of yards across a massive field. We also interviewed some of the recruits and heard their gritty stories. But the most impressive part of the trip was the graduation ceremony for those who had completed the grueling camp. They were smartly dressed in full uniform, marching in tight line and cadence. I could feel honor and pride on display. These recruits could now own the title of Marines. They were warriors ready to serve their country, even if it meant giving their lives.

Here lies the strength of a warrior. It comes from his willingness to let his life go for the sake of something higher. He submits his masculine energy to that which is greater than himself, to something both transcendent and honorable. Then he exercises that submission by offering his skill and courage to those in need around him. Picture a lazy river that gets funneled into a narrow gorge of rock. The slow drift of the current becomes a raging torrent. Its strength can now smash canoes, mangle swimmers, and erode the very rock that gave it such strength. Such water is to be feared. When a man submits to a purpose greater than himself, his own strength becomes just as fearsome.

This was brought home to me while reading the memoirs of a former Army Delta Force officer, titled *The Mission, the Men, and Me*. During the chaos of war, he found three guiding principles that were the key to making life-and-death decisions on the battlefield. First, he had to keep clear about the mission he was on.

Everything had to serve the purpose for which he was sent. Second, he had to think about the men under his command: "Take care of your men's welfare by listening and leading them with sound tactics and techniques that accomplish your mission and always have the courage to do the right things by them." He was their leader, but he would lead by setting an example and serving their needs in battle. Finally, there was himself. Yes, he had to take care of himself, but only after thinking about the first two: "Never put your own personal well-being or advancement ahead of the accomplishment of your mission and taking care of your men."[12] The posture of a servant isn't some feeble, religious ideal. It isn't for men who can't stand up for themselves or who have no voice of their own. It isn't impotence and weakness. It's the guts and grit of being a warrior.

A warrior-servant lives and dies by the quest with which he fully aligns himself. This mission will always involve sacrificing for the benefit of others. Every tale that has ever captured a man's heart has a hero like this. Around December 7 each year, Heidi and I watch the movie *Pearl Harbor* as a way to honor the sacrifices of so many men during World War II. The turning point of the movie, as well as the war on the Pacific front, happened with the Doolittle Raid, a crazy, nearly suicidal mission of sixteen planes and eighty flyers who snuck into Japan in 1942 and bombed Tokyo and surrounding areas. A few of them never made it back. They volunteered for this, fully aligning themselves with the mission, in the hope that it would serve their country and win the war. Although the physical damage inflicted was minimal compared to the catastrophe at Pearl Harbor, the psychological toll was devastating. For the first time, Japan realized it wasn't invincible, and American morale was boosted. Those eighty men submitted to the mission and offered what they could to America. It turned the tide of the war.

A warrior-servant finds his strength not by climbing on top of others or wielding angry tirades. He finds it not by a power-grab, but by a power-release. He lets himself go for the sake of the mission. He lets himself go for the sake of others. This is his greatness and glory as a man.

THE GREAT WARRIOR-SERVANT

This path to greatness is confirmed by the great Warrior-Servant Himself. The subject of greatness came to the forefront during a heated debate among His disciples (Mark 10:35–45). It all started when James and John came to Jesus with a request. They had experienced His miraculous powers, His incisive teaching, and His magnetic hold on the people. With messianic hopes swirling during that time, they were convinced He was the One, the anointed King who would set up a new golden age for Israel. Jesus Himself seemed to hint that He was. They were so close to the One who would possess the power that goes with kingship, and James and John wanted a piece of it. So they asked Jesus for the seats of honor next to Him, at His right and left, when He came to the throne. The other ten disciples heard about this and were furious. What about them? They wanted a piece of the action too. With tension hanging in the air, Jesus called them together to set them straight.

He first began with a reminder: "You know that those who are regarded as rulers of the Gentiles lord it over them, and their high officials exercise authority over them" (v. 42). Israel at that time was occupied territory under the thumb of the hated Romans with Tiberias Caesar as emperor. They maintained their power by brutal force, inciting fear into those they conquered. Anyone who rebelled was guilty of insurrection and crucified. The terrible torture of such a death was done in a public arena as a further warning to any who thought of revolting. The Romans stayed on top by crushing everyone underneath them. Yet those same leaders whom the disciples despised were the very ones they were imitating.

What is so instructive is how Jesus confronted their lust for power: "Not so with you. Instead, whoever wants to become great among you must be your servant, and whoever wants to be first must be slave of all" (vv. 43–44). He didn't squelch the longing for greatness, just how they went about it. They were after it the same way men have sought it over the centuries: by force, conquest, and domination. Jesus' way is startling. It's none of that. You become great by lifting up the greatness of everyone else.

In one sense, this idea is new. In another sense, it's what we've known all along. Such is the wonder we feel with heroes. When a man risks his life to save others, what else is that but lifting up their greatness at his expense? Every military organization honors such men with awards and commendations. But we don't need to join the military to become heroic. Jesus said we can enter this greatness now.

If this were not enough, He closed his comments with this: "For even the Son of Man did not come to be served, but to serve, and to give his life as a ransom for many" (v. 45). Great heroes go first and open the way for others to follow. This is the greatness of Jesus. He went first, doing what no one else could do. His forfeited life would open the prison doors of death and smash the bonds of sin and shame. The great Warrior-Servant had a mission to accomplish, and nothing was going to stop Him, not even the horror of a Roman cross. Jesus wielded His strength in an unparalleled show of no force. The King let Himself go. He did it to serve us. In doing so, He honored the greatness inside each one of us.

We are so valuable that we are worth dying for.

ENTERING THE SECRET

We come now to a surprising turn in the heroic journey. The fierce love that drove Jesus to His death calls for a response from us. It's a response more pivotal than answering the call of the quest to serve others. We must first let ourselves be served by Him.

There is hesitation, even embarrassment, at such an idea. These same feelings pervaded the disciples the night before Jesus died. He did something unimaginable in their eyes, unthinkable for a king (John 13:2–17). He stripped down to a loincloth, as a slave would dress. He took a long towel and wrapped Himself in part of it, keeping the rest free to dry the disciples' feet. Then He went around to each of them, washing and drying their feet, a customary service done by slaves to guests upon entering a home. The shock of such a gesture left them speechless until Peter objected. Only after some coaxing from Jesus did he allow his own feet to be washed. When Jesus had finished, He explained Himself: "You call me 'Teacher' and 'Lord,' and rightly so, for that is what I am. Now that I, your Lord and Teacher, have washed your feet, you also should wash one another's feet" (vv. 13–14).

We enter the secret of heroic greatness by allowing Jesus to serve us first. In one sense, this has already been happening. Every breath you take comes from the One who holds the keys to your life and death. Every motion you make toward Him is only responding to His initiative. You have been unknowingly served by Him from the moment you entered this world. Now you are asked to consciously receive that service. You are asked to receive His fierce love for you.

This may be the hardest task a man faces. When I coached track, I would work with the sprinters on the finer points of running at maximal speed. There were certain form cues they had to master, but the most important one of all was also the biggest challenge. The key to running at top speed is total relaxation. It looks like a complete contradiction. Most young sprinters muscle down and grit their teeth to run faster, but it's the surest way to throw a race. Only when the body is totally relaxed can the legs turn over at their swiftest. I would work with my team using 30m sprints. Each one they did would offer a different place to relax: the legs, the torso, the hands, the arms, the face, and then all over. Some sprinters would master the technique in one season, but most would need more time to get the feel of it. It took intentional effort to relax.

I can think of no better analogy to our situation. Men scavenge for greatness like a bunch of green sprinters. They muscle down and clench their teeth, feeling that if they can chase the winning prize long enough and hard enough, they can win it. But the prize eludes them.

Jesus' way is so opposite. The greatest effort a man must expend is to rest in His love. The greatest challenge is to let himself be served by the Master. But when a man is determined to go here, he will know that Jesus knows him. A man who feels so honored by the great Warrior-Servant will be the man who is free to serve others.

LIVING THE SECRET

I have a good friend who has been a lifelong pastor. During our walks together, one of his prayers is this: "May we be like the high tide. Everyone rises up around us, and nobody knows why." Yes, that's the spirit of the warrior-servant. Here is another image I have always loved. Imagine an oasis in a barren desert. There is lush greenery all around, a striking contrast to the rest of the landscape. You hear water babbling from a spring-fed stream. You see grasses at the water's edge growing tall. You hear the chipping of cardinals as they flutter about. Everything is flourishing around you. You feel drawn to stay and explore this striking wonder surrounded by such desolation. You sense that if you stay here long enough, you will start to flourish as well. This image is a picture of the warrior-servant. Everything flourishes around him.

But the man bent on grabbing at his own greatness is just another Ozymandius. History is wearied to death with such men. They repeat the same tiresome story of trampling on others to look great. There is no flourishing, just decay and death. But the heroic way is the cutting edge of redemption. It is a man's entrance into noble stature: "The noble make noble plans, and by noble deeds they stand" (Isa. 32:8). What are those noble plans? What are those noble deeds? They are plans to help. They are deeds to serve. You become noble right where you are, starting with those closest to you.

For many men, it begins with their marriage. Whatever struggles or disappointments a man has felt here, the determination to serve is ground zero for restoration. Women live with carefully guarded hearts—and for good reason. The beauty of a woman's soul is easily tarnished and vandalized. The violations a woman endures, especially at the hands of other men, compel her to hide that beauty. But the noble husband finds a way to unlock her soul. He finds a key. He becomes a warrior for her soul, offering what he has without demanding a certain response. In doing so, he practices the heroic love Paul envisioned: "Husbands, love your wives, just as Christ loved the church and gave himself up for her" (Eph. 5:25).

Noble plans and deeds also include a man's family. From my years in the classroom, I could quickly differentiate students who had attentive fathers from those who with absentee ones. The former emanated a quiet security and solidity. They still dealt with the same challenges and inner doubts as their peers, but their fathers acted as a shield. Those challenges didn't upend them. Those inner doubts didn't define them. They knew the attentive care of a father who had played with them on the swings or coached them on the ball field. They had flourished in his presence.

The noble plans to serve can also happen in the workplace, the local church, and the community, whether a man is married or single. He can become that high tide that lifts everyone up. He can become that oasis in the desert.

I had the honor of serving beside such a man as a colleague for a number of years. Ben was the high school's Latin teacher. It's hard to think of a more difficult subject to make appealing for that age group. But somehow he did it. The magic wasn't his teaching methods or incisive intellect. The magic was Ben. Students loved him. They flourished under his tutelage.

During my last year of teaching, we shared a room together, but only for part of that year. He started having difficulty swallowing, and by Christmas, had been diagnosed with esophageal cancer. The downhill track from there was swift. The school wrestled with the situation. How could this happen to such a beloved teacher? As he approached the end, the entire high school boarded buses one school morning and came to his home to sing worship songs outside his window. Those same songs had been a ballast for his soul during the whole ordeal. One of his children took a short video of the event. It went viral online, seen by more than forty million viewers. Ben had always prayed that his sickness could advance the Kingdom. It did so in a way he could have never imagined.

His funeral may be the most remarkable one I have ever attended. The large sanctuary was packed. Students, friends, and colleagues came to honor the one who had so honored them. One by one, they came up and shared their stories of how he had served them in some surprising way. One that still haunts me came from a friend who lived in Ben's neighborhood. He described going through a time of terrible hardship and Ben's startling way of serving him. For almost three months, Ben would appear at his door and knock. Upon answering, Ben would hug him, say that he loved him, then turn and walk away. No response was ever asked for. The friend never knew when the daily knock would come, but it never failed to arrive. Sometimes Ben would show up in pajamas in the early morning, sometimes in professional attire for school, sometimes in sweats on the weekend. That knock was what got him through the ordeal.

When all the stories had been told and the final hymn sung, I didn't want to leave the funeral. I wanted to stay and hear more. In the sorrow of losing Ben, I had also felt awe. I had witnessed the legacy of a heroic man.

Men scheme for fame and prestige because they are terrified of failure. But the man who serves can never fail. Ben's life was proof. His greatness is one any man can attain.

CHAPTER 13

ENTERING
THE SILENCE

*"The present state of the world and the whole of
life is diseased. If I were a doctor and were asked
for my advice, I should reply, 'Create silence.'"*
—Søren Kirkegaard, *Self-Examination/Judge for
Yourselves*

*"We too are called to withdraw at certain intervals
into deeper silence and aloneness with God,
together as a community as well as personally;
to be alone with Him—not with our books,
thoughts, and memories but completely stripped
of everything—to dwell lovingly in His presence,
silent, empty, expectant, and motionless."*
—Mother Teresa, *In the Heart of the World*

*But the Lord is in his holy temple; let all
the earth keep silence before him.*
—Habakkuk 2:20 ESV

We are now approaching the end of our journey through
the heroic, but questions still hang in the air. They're
the practical ones: How does man start this journey?
How does he learn to receive Jesus' personal coaching?
How does he walk through his initiation? How does he
detach and unmask? How does he find his true name

and receive his quest? How does he submit himself as a warrior who serves? How does he become heroic and find his truest manhood? I discovered the answer to all of these questions in the last place I ever expected. Here's how it happened:

During my time as a high school Bible teacher, I taught a basic manhood class to sophomores and juniors. We waded through many of the issues laid out in this book. They learned to share their stories and trust each other as brothers. But I also wanted to give them an opportunity to connect to God in a meaningful way. The classroom seemed too sterile for this, so I came up with an idea. I would take the school bus and drive them to a quiet spot in the woods at a nearby park. Here I would give them each a Bible and a couple of verses to look up. The instructions were simple: *Find a place in the woods where you are alone and spend fifteen minutes in silence. Then come back when you hear the sound of the bus horn.* The whole thing was a huge risk. Imagine releasing a classroom of boys into the woods with no supervision after being cooped up in school. You can come up with your own disaster story. So did I. But the disasters never happened (except for one student who got lost in the woods). After the fifteen minutes were over and they came back to the bus, we would spend time debriefing. Over and over, I would hear them comment about how meaningful the time was. Some experienced a settled peace amid the stresses of school. Some heard the sounds of nature as never before. Some became aware of their hearts in a new way. Still others were suddenly attuned to God's presence. Years later, I still hear from students who speak about how pivotal those fifteen minutes were. The trips to the park were the most important thing that ever happened to them in the class. Ironically, no one was talking to them. No one was asking them to do anything. No one was expecting anything from them. They were alone and still and quiet.

They had entered the silence.

CHASING AND RUNNING

We live in a world that stakes its existence on noise and busyness. The hundreds of TV stations, millions of YouTube clips, and countless talk shows and podcasts create an onslaught of sound. Add to that the incessant conversations via email, text, or social media. Finish this off with our frantic lifestyles, propelled by work pressures and modern family life. We think that life is found here, that this is where this action is. We are deceived.

I suspect that if all the noise and busyness stopped for one hour, most of what we call civilization would come crashing down into an unrecognizable heap. We know how to do noise. We know how to do busy. But silence? What is that? When I meet men for the first time and start talking about our jobs, I sometimes like to say that I take men into silence. I get some odd looks or an awkward pause in the conversation. It doesn't fit any category. Who does silence?

But silence is where the action is. I firmly believe that our chief sin as men has nothing to do with our rampant sexual issues of whatever stripe or color. It's our busyness. And it's killing us. For most of us, I suspect that all the busyness and noise are bound up in our chase for false glory. Even more damning, I suspect that we are running away from something else. Men get edgy when they think about entering silence. They aren't being asked to do something or become something. No one is looking at them, and there is nothing to prove. Their whole sense of being has been chained to motion and striving, but it now all comes to an ominous stop. They are alone and stripped of pretense. What surfaces now is fear—the fear of nothingness. When a man feels this, he is on the verge of greatness. He is on the verge of meeting God.

THE POWER OF SILENCE

So much has been written about the benefits of silence. Psychologically, it can promote self-discovery and mindfulness. Emotionally, it can be a potent stress reliever and increase empathy with others. Mentally, it has been shown to improve memory and problem-solving skills. Physically, it can fight off insomnia and potentially grow brain cells. There are even neurological studies that show the impact of silence on brain structure. However interesting all of that is, there is something much more important at stake.

Undergirding the entire story of the Bible are two massive realities: God is always present and He is always working. All of our dysfunctions as men flow from our inability to live in these two realities. All of our fear and striving, all of our addictions and neuroses, all of our thoughtless acts and petty sins come out of a felt vacuum at our core. If only we could somehow access His presence. If only we could somehow sense His activity. But how does this happen? How do these two realities stain a man's soul? How do they replace the inner void that betrays him and binds him to narcissism? There is only one place it happens: in the silence.

I know this for certain from my own story. Take the lust for fame I have already recounted. It betrayed me for decades. No matter how I pushed it down or shoved it into a closet, it would escape to haunt me again. What I haven't told is how the lust was extinguished. My own entrance into silence began to happen on my back porch each morning. Here, amid the retreating darkness and the chatter of the wrens, I learned to come before God. I had already learned much about opening the Bible to read and ponder a passage. It took me much longer to open my heart. Under all the layers of pretense and shame, submerged anger and grief, I found desire, stinging desire—a hissing cauldron of lust coercing me to seek fame. But in the silence, something unexpected happened. I discovered that my lust was not evil. It was just misplaced. The stinging desire was to be known and affirmed. What little fame I had achieved never quenched the desire and only fanned the lust. Now the real surprise came. As I was looking for God and for my heart in all of this, I experienced something, at first so subtle that it vanished as soon as I noticed it. I felt that He was looking at me. It may be hard to believe, but trust me, it's much harder to describe. I just knew that His eye was upon me. I knew that I was known by Him and affirmed by Him. In that moment of being seen, the lust disappeared. I didn't try to make it go away. It just vaporized when I saw Him seeing me. But it only happened in the silence.

BECOMING HEROIC IN THE SILENCE

The heroic journey in all the great myths begins with a period of separation or departure. Here the hero leaves his familiar surroundings and hears the call to adventure that forms the beginning of his quest. Here he also meets a mentor to guide him and leaves the ordinary world he has known to be prepared for his mission. It occurred to me one day that this is exactly what happens in the silence. We intentionally take ourselves out of the ordinary world of deadlines, text messages, and to-do lists. We leave the busyness and noise that envelopes us and enter the silence. This is how a man starts out and continues on the heroic journey. This is where he learns to hear the coaching of the living Christ. This is where he finds the strength to persevere through the tests of detaching and unmasking. This is where he receives his new name and discovers his quest. And this is where he receives the strength to persevere on the quest despite opposition, roadblocks, and failure. None of this will happen in the noise. It won't happen in the busyness. You won't walk the heroic path by watching another hero at the movies or by reading about one in a story. You won't even walk it by reading this book.

A man becomes heroic only in the silence.

Take the life of the Great Hero. He began His ministry in silence. After being baptized by his cousin John, He was driven into the wilderness by the Holy Spirit. The forty days in the wilderness were an intense period of separation. He departed from all that He had known to be tested physically by a fast during the whole time. He was also tempted by Satan himself. The tests and temptations were necessary to prepare Him for a quest no man had ever taken—to conquer sin and death itself. In the wilderness, He was learning to say no to the great deceiver. He was learning to wield His strength for others, not for Himself. He was learning to depend on His Father. And it all happened with no human eye watching. It happened in the silence.

Silence was a part of His daily life as well. After He came back from those forty days and called His first disciples, the gospel of Mark recounts a day in the life of Jesus (Mark 1:21–38). He taught in the local synagogue with astonishing authority, not quoting other rabbis as most teachers did, but simply making startling pronouncements. He then backed up His words with deeds, casting out an evil spirit and healing Peter's mother-in-law. In one day, the atomic blast of His presence spread ripples everywhere. By nightfall, a throng of the sick and demon-possessed were being brought to Him. In fact, the whole town of Capernaum was now assembled at the home in which he was staying. The quest had started. But the separation that began in the wilderness continued.

Here's how Mark puts it: "Then, in the early morning, while it was still dark, Jesus got up, left the house and went off to a deserted place, and there he prayed" (1:35 PHILLIPS). Before the noise and busyness began again, before the hustle of the crowds and the battles with the demonic, Jesus entered silence. He went before the first rays of sunlight, when no eye was watching, and found a deserted place. The word for *deserted place* could also be translated as *wilderness place*. Yet there was no wilderness geographically around Capernaum. It was all cultivated land. The inference is that it was a wilderness place metaphorically, like the wilderness of His temptations, a place of silence and aloneness. There He communed with His Father. There He felt His identity as a beloved Son. And there He received strength to continue the quest that would take Him to the cross. He separated from the world to enter the silence. Now He could reenter the world and continue the mission.

Stop for a moment and take in Jesus' example. He was becoming headline news. The buzz about Him was everywhere. So many thought He was to be the next great king of Israel. His life became a flurry of activity for the next three years. But the real activity happened in that deserted place when no one was watching. As our Coach and Captain, we are to follow in His path.

STORIES OF THE SILENCE

I have watched the power of silence repeatedly in my work with men in spiritual direction. Here, I sit with a man and help him discern how God is working in his life and how he can respond to Him. But we don't start in conversation. We start in silence. As awkward as it may seem at first to sit in silence for a few minutes, men come to love the time. They pause, unburden, pray, and listen. I am astonished at how often what needs to be addressed comes up in the silence. The deeper issues of the heart have a chance to surface. And they begin to hear His voice. One man came to me sick of living with the pressure of having to prove himself to others. As we entered the silence, he suddenly heard, "Come. I'm here." It was a gentle invitation from the Lord. But it took some time for him to learn to come. During another time in the silence, an image came to him of a long-forgotten memory: he was sitting in his father's lap as a young boy. He could recall the sensation, the smell, and the feel of that security. This was followed by other times when he began to rest in the Father's love using the memory of that image. He was learning to be a beloved son. He was learning to come. It only happened in the silence.

The work of spiritual direction also involves helping a person structure daily silence with God. Men often tell me that they are terrible with silence. The mind wanders. The heart is agitated. The pressures of the world intrude. Then they feel bad that they can't do silence. It's easy to give up if it feels like another pass/ fail performance. But all of this is a part of learning to separate from the world and enter the silence. It takes time to learn to slow down. It takes time to go inward. It takes time to allow desire to surface. And it takes time to hear Him.

Extended times of quiet are also helpful for the heroic journey. I take small groups of men to a local retreat center for a day of silence. All phones and computers are left in the car. The only thing allowed is a Bible and a journal. After some suggestions for Scripture and prayer, we enter the silence together. There in the quiet, Jesus faithfully comes to each man, giving him what he needs. On one of those retreats, a man came struggling with a very difficult health issue in one of his children. He had always dealt with sadness in his life by immediately running to a possible happy ending so he could explain how it's all going to work out. But there was no resolution in sight for this situation with his child. As he walked the retreat grounds, he sensed Jesus telling him, "Let's stay in the struggle." It gave him permission to be present with both his grief and joy, opening up a brand-new place inside of him to be present with himself and the Lord.

Another man came with a heart-wrenching story of physical and sexual abuse as a boy. As he sat out in the sun to be still and pray, he closed his eyes and noticed the colors being triggered on the inside of his eyelids after seeing the sunlight. A memory then surfaced of being in the first grade when he was taught the primary colors. He remembered the wonder of being enchanted by the beauty of those three simple colors. There was no hypervigilance from the all the abuse, only an openness of heart to receive. It was then that he sensed Jesus calling out that first-grade boy to come and receive the love He could offer. It's the boy Jesus wanted, the boy who had gone into hiding all those years to survive.

I have countless stories like these, enough to fill another book. They all show the power of silence, attesting to how the Lord will meet a man when he chooses to withdraw from the world. Some of the stories are dramatic and create massive shifts in a man's soul. Other stories are quieter, demonstrating the Lord's slow and steady work. A man may not receive what he thinks he must have, but he always receives what he truly needs.

I have told a few of the stories in this book of how Jesus has met me in the silence. Through attuning to my heart and to the words of Scripture, I have experienced both the breakthrough shifts and the quieter moments. But the most transforming prayer for me has become the prayer of surrender. Here, I drop all of my ponderings and prayers and simply sit in His presence. As thoughts come to mind of whatever sort, whether good or bad, I just surrender them and return to the silence. Something happens in that surrender that has never happened before. I am communing with Him and feel His presence entering into the subconscious landscapes of my heart. I sense His love flowing into all that is me, both the known and the unknown to me, both the flawed and good. In that love, I am becoming my true self, my own man. In that love, He is also making me like Himself.

THE FINAL GLORY

If a man stays with the silence long enough, something else will happen that he will hardly notice. It is the prize that has eluded him all his life. Athletes compete to win it. Soldiers fight to achieve it. All men strive to gain it. It is glory. It is the aura of the hero. What has always eluded them, Jesus now comes to give them: "I have given them the glory that you gave me . . ." (John 17:22). The glory that was lost in the garden is the same glory He comes to plant in the heart of a man. You are not your shame and fear. You are not your sins and idols. You are not your biggest mistakes or your worst moments. He sees you as something so much more. He wants you to taste the glory of being a man and begin offering that to others. It is this motion that will cause the world to pause in wonder and realize that Jesus is the truth.

You are also destined for something so much more: "I consider that our present sufferings are not worth comparing with the glory that will be revealed in us" (Rom. 8:18). Now in this present life, there will be many perils. The heroic quest will always mean some kind of suffering. Some of us may be called to places of great struggle or opposition. We may experience failure or rejection—or even death. Despite all of this, we will be asked to continue to serve and seek the good of all around us, including our persecutors. We are to carry on this way until physical death takes us or the great Hero returns. But rest assured, His glory one day will burn inside of us. It will emanate in a splendor so solid that we will wonder how we could have ever existed without such realness. In that place, we won't need any more heroic stories. We won't need any more heroes.

We will be gazing at Him.

And we will see Him gazing at us.

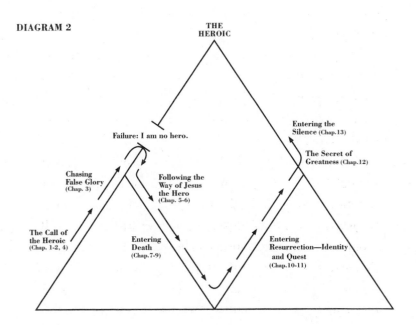

DIAGRAM 2

THE
HEROIC

Failure: I am no hero.

Entering the
Silence (Chap. 13)

The Secret of
Greatness (Chap. 12)

Chasing
False Glory
(Chap. 3)

Following the
Way of Jesus
the Hero
(Chap. 5-6)

The Call of
the Heroic
(Chap. 1-2, 4)

Entering
Death
(Chap. 7-9)

Entering
Resurrection—Identity
and Quest
(Chap. 10-11)

Here is the same diagram from the introduction, but now the chapters are included to show the flow of the book. We can only reach the heroic after entering the death and resurrection of Jesus. Only the Great Hero can guide us on this path, His path into true manhood.

NOTES

1. *The Father Effect*, directed by John Finch (FaithWorks, 2017).

2. Humphrey Carpenter, *J. R. R. Tolkien: A Biography* (New York: Houghton Mifflin Company, 2000), 197–98.

3. "Hero Maker," *Christianity Today*, Oct. 18, 2006.

4. "Running the Race," *Christianity Today*, Oct. 5, 2010.

5. Ibid.

6. "Hero Maker," *Christianity Today*, Oct. 18, 2006.

7. J. R. R. Tolkien, *On Fairy-Stories*, www.excellence-in-literature.com/wp-content/uploads/2013/10/fairysto-riesbytolkien.pdf, 23.

8. George MacDonald, *Lilith* (New York: Ballantine Books, 1969), 35.

9. Ibid., 239.

10. *The Heart of Man*, directed by Eric Esau (Gather Films, 2017).

11. J. R. Tolkien, *The Return of the King: Being the Third Part of The Lord of the Rings* (Boston, MA: Mariner Books, 2012), 140.

12. Pete Blaber, *The Mission, the Men, and Me: Lessons from a Former Delta Force Commander* (New York: Dutton Caliber, 2008), 11.

WHICH TRAIL TO CHOOSE NEXT?

You have reached the end of *Heroic*, but that's just the beginning. You are at the trailhead of something wild and good and epic. Do you want to keep going forward? Here are some different trails to start walking down. Choose one and move out:

- **Get a copy of the Expedition Guide to *Heroic*,** a guided tour through the book. You can use the questions for journaling. Better still, grab a small group of men and use the Expedition Guide to start a conversation about manhood and the heroic longing. Download at HeroicBook.com.

- **Find a mentor, an older man you admire** and ask him to read the book with you. Take a chapter at a time and talk about it. Ask him about his story and be willing to tell him yours.

- **Go to LandmarkJourneyMinistries.com** and sign up to receive Bill's weekly blog post. He will continue to write about the ideas in *Heroic* so that you can remember and reorient. In return you will receive his free *Trail Guide into Manhood*, a 30-day devotional.

- **Enter the Silence.** Finally, the heroic journey is all about finding a guide, owning an identity, and discovering a quest. Jesus can be our guide, offer us an identity, and give us a quest. He wants to coach us into all of this, and we learn best about that coaching in the silence. Go to landmarkjourneyministries.com and look for upcoming *Heroic* retreats that will help you enter the silence.

Connect to Bill and Landmark Journey Ministries through social media:

 @BillDelvaux billdelvaux

LandmarkJourneyMinistries.com

ASK BILL
TO COME SPEAK
to your men's group
or lead your men's retreat.

Contact Bill at LandmarkJourneyMinistries.com